The story behind television's most popular country music program

by **CLIFFORD ENDRES**   **Photographs by Scott Newton and others**

AUSTIN CITY LIMITS

UNIVERSITY OF TEXAS PRESS, AUSTIN

First edition, 1987

Requests for permission
to reproduce material from
this work should be sent to:
    Permissions
    University of Texas Press
    Box 7819
    Austin, Texas 78713-7819

Library of Congress
Cataloging-in-Publication Data

Endres, Clifford, 1941–
    Austin city limits.

    Bibliography: p.
    Includes index.
    1. Austin city limits (Television program).
2. Country music — United States — History
and criticism.   3. Western swing (Music) —
United States — History and criticism.
I. Newton, Scott.   II. Title.
ML3524.E5   1987   784.5′2′00973 86-27215
ISBN 0-292-70378-3
ISBN 0-292-70398-8 (pbk.)

Four lines from "London Homesick Blues"
reprinted by permission of Gary P. Nunn.

Photographs from Seasons 1–4
are by Austin City Limits staff photographers,
including Lance Moreland, Janet Bandy,
and David Eberhardt
Photographs from Seasons 5–11
are by Scott Newton unless otherwise
indicated.
All photographs edited by Scott Newton.

To the Musicians

ORIGINALLY this book was intended to be published as part of *Austin City Limits'* tenth anniversary celebration, which has meanwhile come and gone. Here, now, is the book: belated, but a tribute nonetheless to a pioneering television series whose subject is music.

Writing about the television show proved impossible, of course, without treating in some fashion its relevance to modern country music in general and southwestern regional music in particular. Regarding the former, over the past decade and a half an extensive bibliography has grown up, and the latter has recently begun to attract serious attention in its own right. The discussion here of country music should not be read as a scholarly treatment, but as simply an attempt to establish a television show in its musical context. Dispensing with footnotes, I have tried to mention in the text everyone from whose work I have drawn, with one large exception. Bill Malone's *Country Music, U.S.A.* occupies more or less the position of the Bible in country music scholarship, and I have depended on it accordingly. For those who want it, a detailed guide to books and articles on country music may be found in Malone's excellent bibliographical essays at the back of his book. Jan Reid's 1974 book on Austin music, *The Improbable Rise of Redneck Rock,* remains the most useful reportage on that cultural phenomenon. A larger book, however, deserves to be written before the period's brief and brilliant flowering fades further from memory.

For graciously contributing their time and attention in interviews, I am grateful to Johnny Gimble, Fred "Papa" Calhoun, Darrell Royal, Floyd Tillman, Joe Gracey, Bobby Earl Smith, Mary-Margaret Byerman, John T. Davis, Townsend Miller, Hugh Sparks, and Ruth Pruett. Help from Austin City Limits staff was indispensable, especially from Bill Arhos, Terry Lickona, David Hough, Susan Caldwell, and Jeff Peterson. ACL alumni Bruce Scafe and Paul Bosner commented frankly and generously. I thank them, and also Howard Chalmers, Allan Muir, Ken Waggoner, and Donn Rogosin.

I wish also to thank these present KLRU and ACL staff and production members for their courteous assistance: María Rodríguez, Mike Archenhold, Michael Emery, Bink Williams, Gene Harris, Bob Selby, Dean Rabourn, Howard Gutin, and the rest of a very friendly company.

A large number of writers on American vernacular music and culture owe considerable thanks to folklorist Archie Green for his energetic encouragement and constructive criticism; I am happy to include myself among them. Part of Archie Green's unflagging message that Austin should take its local culture seriously seems to have borne fruit, for the Barker Texas History Center at the University of Texas at Austin has established a Sound Archives which includes a Texas music collection and memorabilia from the Armadillo era. We are grateful to John Wheat, Archives Coordinator, for his assistance in providing posters and other illustrations.

I must also thank the Turkish-American Association in Izmir, Turkey, where I had the great pleasure of spending a year as a Fulbright scholar, for their hospitality in kindly allowing me to type the final draft on their sleek typewriter. Finally, a tip of the hat to Joe E. Brown, Jr., requiescat in pace, who knew about Willie before Willie was cool.

C. E.
May 1986

Gary Morris

I

T'S TWO IN THE AFTERNOON, and rehearsal for the first Austin City Limits taping of 1985 is getting under way. The huge sixth-floor studio at KLRU-TV envelops you. Outside, the temperature is 101°, normal for August, and the Austin lawns lie brown and parched in the blazing sun. The studio, however, is dark and cool, chilled by tons of air-conditioning equipment. Here you are in a separate world. You do not hear sounds of traffic or sirens or cicadas whirring in the hot afternoon. Heavy black drapes cover the windowless walls. The only light emanates from batteries of high-powered spotlights that hang by cables from the ceiling and pour their artificial luminescence down on a wooden stage and bleachers. A cycloramic backdrop that closely resembles Austin's nighttime skyline circles behind the stage and into the wings. Clumps of small trees and ferns in pots, looking unnaturally fresh and green in the yellow-tinged light, ornament the space. The vaporous, cool, aquarium-like atmosphere is beginning, you think, to affect your grip on reality. Then you remember that the business of these people is to change reality, to create illusion, to make magic. And you're in their workshop.

From a low hum and buzz the sound level in the studio rises to a medium roar. Technicians swarm over the stage crowded with musical instruments, amplifiers, and microphones. They raise and lower lights, replace bulbs, patch wires into the lighting console in the control room. The sound crew strings cables and checks wiring, trying to get a buzz out of the system. Crisp directives punctuate the din.

"Bring in M. Take up K. Stand by." The voice belongs to lighting director Bob Selby, in the headset and antennae, looking like everyone's favorite Martian. This is Austin City Limits' eleventh season, and Selby has been here from the beginning. He is said to be the best in the business.

"Can I hear some kick drum? Can I hear kick and snare?" This time the voice comes over the studio speakers from the audio director, David Hough. Also part of the show since its beginning, Hough is a skinny guy of forty with a balding head and a twinkle in his eye. Back in the audio room, out of sight, he plugs into the action through his own wires and headset.

A small crowd begins to populate the bleachers: studio hangers-on, the band's friends and roadies, a few curious students. Things are running about fifty minutes behind schedule. The crew finishes the sound check, and the studio cameras, looking like fugitive robots from *Star Wars,* roll into the room for a camera check. The cameramen rehearse their moves and practice various shots, warming up and easing back into the groove after a long five months' lay-off.

Through the swirling eddies and currents of activity a skinny, frizzy-haired man threads his way, wearing a mask of complete unflappability, talking to this person, answering that question, applying the glue to hold things together. This is Terry Lickona, since 1978 the show's producer. In that time Lickona has evolved into one of the industry's most highly respected music producers. With him at the reins Austin City Limits has flourished, achieving in recent years a popular and critical success that no one familiar with its origins would have dreamed of.

Finally, the band is ready to take the stage. The singer and star is Gary Morris, born and raised in Fort Worth, Texas, now a country-pop success in Nashville, where he has cut four albums and been nominated for Male Vocalist of the Year. Recently he sang the male lead in *La Bohème*, opposite Linda Ronstadt, in a New York Shakespeare Festival production. *Rolling Stone* likes him. The *New York Times* likes him. Country music has changed a lot in the last ten years. Who knows? Gary Morris may be the wave of the future.

A guitarist in the band looks around the studio and muses, "I watched this show for years. Before we played on it, I always thought it was shot outside."

The band's sound man says, "This show is like a dream, compared to Nashville television. It's the only one that gives a damn about the audio. Here we can do it our way."

In the audio control room, as a matter of fact, there are a few problems. Some pops, buzzes, and hums refuse to go away. The room itself looks like Frankenstein's laboratory: snarls and coils of wire, meters with quivering needles, gauges, dots of light that glow and blink, tape reels and screwdrivers and pliers and electronic tubes lying about in wanton disarray. The technicians huddle animatedly, trying and discarding one solution after another, oblivious to the lovely women smiling from the advertising posters taped to the walls.

In front of the stage, Gary Menotti, the show's director, pulls a chair up to a small café table and sits facing the band. Menotti is a stocky fellow with curly hair and beard, wearing jeans and T-shirt and a big smile. He's been director for the last four years. Cameraman Mike Archenhold, who doubles as Menotti's assistant director, joins him. Rehearsal finally begins, an hour and a half behind schedule. Nobody much minds; it's not bad for the first shoot. Menotti lays a stopwatch on the table and pulls out a sheet of paper. He will time the band's songs and each musician's solos, note changes of instrument and position, and think about interesting camera shots. The charts he makes now will establish the game plan for tonight.

Rehearsal ends. At 5:00 a beer truck arrives to unload four kegs and a dozen cases of Budweiser. In season eight, Bud replaced Lone Star as the chief underwriter and beer supplier for the show. By 7:00 studio audience ticket holders begin riding the elevators to the sixth floor, where they'll drink beer and mill around happily until the show starts.

Standing among them with plastic beer cup in hand, turning upon the proceedings a fond and vaguely proprietary gaze not unlike that of a host at a dinner party or a father viewing a game of tag among rowdy children, is Bill Arhos. Currently executive producer, Arhos has been identified with Austin City Limits longer than anyone else in the room. Without him, in fact, the show would probably not exist: Not only did he hatch the original idea, but it was his single-minded determination that more than once brought the series back from the brink of financial extinction. Arhos sips his beer and looks content.

At 8:00 P.M. Lickona takes the stage. He delivers brief instructions to the audience. "Have fun, and don't hold anything back. If you have to leave, do it between songs, and watch out for those cameras. Now let's have an Austin City Limits welcome for Gary Morris."

In the video control room Gary Menotti hovers expectantly before a formidable bank of television screens. These and the speaker monitors connect him to what's happening in the studio. A console board bristles with levers and dials; Ed "Fast Eddie" Fuentes, the show's technical director, mans the controls. Menotti paces the floor like a caged bear, tethered to

1985 Austin City Limits poster

the console by his headset, charts in hand. He makes large and theatrical gestures, as though his cameramen two rooms away could see him.

"Are we ready on two? I'm rolling tape." To Audio: "Are you rolling tape? Hey, we're burning daylight, let's get it on. Let me know when you're rolling, Recording."

The band builds the tension with a forty-five second overture, and suddenly everything is alive. Gary Morris is leaning into the microphone, his band is hot, the tapes are rolling, and Gary Menotti is dancing in the video room with the image streams from five cameras.

"Hold your shot, Mike. Give me that guitar, Doug, on your left. Stand by, Mike. Okay, you got it. Tight, tight, tight! Give me a shot on three. . . . Dissolve three. Stand by, five. . . . Beautiful! Hold your shots, guys. Nice shot, nice shot, Robert. Good show, guys, you're doin' good."

At first the crew members feel a little creaky as they work out the kinks. But halfway along, they begin to loosen up; the half-forgotten rhythms return, the jitters dissolve. The band is rocking. The studio camera operators — Mike Archenhold, Doug Robb, and Michael Emery — waltz their mechanical partners through the crowd in smooth, fluid moves, dipping and bending as they home in on the stage with practiced instinct. Robert Moorehead, handheld camera at the ready, hovers at the stage apron while crane cameraman Vance Holmes focuses in from his vantage point on the boom of the serenely circling vehicle. Smelling out the right publicity shot, still photographer Scott Newton bobs and weaves and manages to dodge the big cameras. The whole affair resembles a slightly demented dance, weirdly choreographed perhaps, but not without its own harmony.

The television monitor screens are Menotti's eyes, his only windows to the studio action. The images on these screens are what he selects and blends into the primary tape, or "rough cut" of the show. A second tape (shot by the crane camera) is kept as a backup; in the final editing, the staff can add alternative shots from this tape to the primary tape to gloss over mistakes, if necessary. This is, of course, not nearly as satisfactory as getting it right the first time.

The director communicates with his cameramen by headset. On both sides, they will try to stay close to the charts they drew up at rehearsal, but everyone has to stay loose all the same. The band may do a song it didn't rehearse; besides, experience has taught that the spontaneous magic of live performance consistently refuses to conform to well-laid plans. When the band veers off from the charts, director and cameramen have to wing it, relying on their sense of one another's expectations and capabilities. As in jazz, invention is generally more exhilarating than playing from charts. Brilliant improvisation, however, is impossible without a comfortable relationship between director and camera operators. Getting good shots depends on being intuitive, loose, and quick. Freezing up can be fatal.

Responding to vocal cues and Menotti's hand signals, Fuentes pushes buttons and flips switches to translate the director's vision into electronic reality. Together they create a rhythm of long shot, medium shot, and close-up; zooms and stationary shots; overhead and floor shots; frames of the performer and cutaways to the audience. Decisions, split-second and irreversible, must be guided by the director's intuition of a smooth and coherent whole. It's very creative work; you can see why nearly every radio-television-film student wants to become a director.

Three-quarters of the way through, it feels like old times again. The timing is sharp, spirits high. A grinning Hough pops into the video control

Scott Newton

room. Mocking Menotti's flamboyant gestures, he winds up and rolls a pantomime bowling ball down an imaginary alley.

Onstage, Gary Morris is working and sweating, and he's got the audience with him. He gets a standing ovation, and returns to sing an aria from *La Bohème* for an encore. It's an astonishing vocal performance, despite a few jokes in the video room about "horse opera." The final fade to black brings handshakes and backslaps all around. The magic words can at last be uttered: "It's on tape."

This is Gary Morris' second appearance on Austin City Limits. His first was two years ago almost to the day. That experience gave him confidence in the staff, so he doesn't bother to watch the playback in the video control room. He's right; it's fine. The staff can go home and relax until Tanya Tucker comes in two nights later.

Tanya Tucker

Like Gary Morris, Tanya Tucker is firmly entrenched in mainstream country music. Her product well illustrates what's coming out of Nashville these days: It's brassy, sexy, boasts a big drum kit and a strong rhythm section, a grand piano and electric keyboards too. The pedal steel man doubles on electric standard guitar, and a lot of his bridges would sound at home on a rock record. Tanya Tucker, except for her Texas twang, might be a pop queen, and that's exactly her ambition. She

and her band have come to Austin from a Las Vegas date to play the Aqua Fest and Austin City Limits.

Tanya and her manager—her father—didn't much want to play Austin City Limits. It doesn't pay much, only union scale; compared to Las Vegas, it's like playing for free. Her reluctance shows: when she takes the stage, she is stiff at first, and not particularly thrilled to be here. But the audience loves her anyway, hooting and hollering and showering her with applause—and she responds. She warms up, starts having fun, forgets about the money, and soon she's belting out songs like there's no tomorrow, working hard, taking chances, letting spontaneity limber up her choreographed Vegas stage movements. By the time she gets to Ed Bruce's "When I Die Just Let Me Go to Texas," she has the crowd in the palm of her hand.

"It's great to be here," she finally says, in a tone of surprise. "This isn't work. It's . . . *play.*"

After her set a crowd of musicians, roadies, friends, and a few refugees from the audience gather in the video control room to watch the playback. It is clear that Tucker, like Morris, has taped a great show. Sometimes television, like the movies, can be a romantic medium. Given the right subject, the camera will caress and flatter it and make it more beautiful than real life. Tanya is a TV natural, and the gaggle in the video room know it. When the tape ends they erupt in raucous cheering, congratulations, and a burst of mutual well-wishing. Someone spills a beer on the big console with the dials and switches. Bink Williams, the "video doctor," grimaces, but not too severely; it's all in a night's work, after all.

Many of the technicians have gone up to the roof to watch the Aqua Fest fireworks on the shore of the Colorado River. An Austin tradition, Aqua Fest is the big-city equivalent of a county fair. The fireworks are spec-

tacular. In the elevator going back down, a young man cresting on Budweiser and mellowness proudly displays Tanya Tucker's autograph on the back of his cheap mimeographed ACL program. For his part, he confides, he has gifted Tanya with his own name, address, and phone number.

The eleventh season of Austin City Limits seems off to a good start. Two shows, two stand-up audiences. No serious problems. A few weeks from now, the director and producer and a small staff will take each tape, edit it down to thirty minutes, and send it out as half of a one-hour program to 286 PBS stations. Next spring Gary Morris and Tanya Tucker will ride an electronic beam into more than ten million living rooms from Alaska to Samoa: a singing picture of mainstream country music in the middle 1980s.

AUSTIN'S MUSICAL STAR was rising dramatically in 1974. The city's premier music hall, Armadillo World Headquarters, was so popular with musicians that national acts would take a cut in pay to play there. The previous summer, Willie Nelson's first official Texas Fourth of July picnic had rocked nearby Dripping Springs. Willie and Waylon Jennings had discovered the basics of love in Luckenbach, Texas, a ghost town not far away in the hill country; thousands of country music fans had responded with ardor for Willie and Waylon and the boys. Michael Martin Murphey had just released an album called *Cosmic Cowboy Souvenir*. A leading local radio station, KOKE-FM, was touting a new style it called "progressive country," a mixture of country and western music laced with rock and blues. The station's logo showed a booted, hatted, long-haired cowboy at the opposite end of a lasso from a recalcitrant goat — a play on "goat roper," the insulting monicker usually applied to Texas ranchers, long shunned by the hip generation as incorrigibly "redneck."

To the great surprise of many, goat roping had suddenly become chic. Not only was it now socially acceptable in Texas' most avant-garde city to drive a beat-up pickup truck to a nightclub and dance there to Marcia Ball's soulful country tunes or Delbert McClinton's whisky-voiced rhythm and blues — it was the preferred mode of transportation. Some wiseacre said the new music sounded like "redneck rock," and the name caught on.

What had happened? This was a direct reversal of the previous decade's attitudes, when the city's young pacesetters, rebelliously rejecting haircuts while embracing rock, folk, and blues, would have preferred to drink muddy water and sleep in a hollow log than betray affinity with their hillbilly cousins. And it looked as if the fun was only starting. Willie Nelson picked up and moved to town lock, stock, and barrel. Jerry Jeff Walker and Michael Murphey did the same. Doug Sahm came back home from San Francisco. Music journalists talked excitedly of "outlaw music," naming Austin as its capital. Musicians themselves daily expressed more disgust with Nashville and what they saw as its fixation with crass commercial values and tired old formulas. Austin was new and fresh. In Austin you could do your own musical thing, and the pickin' lasted all night. In a single evening, for instance, you could have caught Little Feat jamming with Linda Ronstadt and Commander Cody at the Armadillo, or Doug Sahm and Herbie Hancock trading licks at Soap Creek Saloon, or nearly a dozen other equally exciting acts at clubs around town.

The place was in ferment. Douglas B. Green, a country music scholar and performer with Riders in the Sky, wrote about the scene: "It is a strange and energy-filled convergence of folk/rock musicians, singers and songwriters who have come to the country life for their inspiration and to country music for a musical base on which to build their own individual styles. It has been happening in the middle-sized, middle-classed, middle-American, middle-Texas town of Austin, the latest, hippest place to be in the music business." Green's emphasis on *country* might have been slightly misplaced. The interest in country was really only part of a large and widespread quest for authentic musical roots beyond any particular style; but he had the right idea about the city's importance.

Not all these indigenous musicians were country pickers. Bob Brown, for example, lead singer of the venerable Austin rock band Conqueroo, pointedly defined country music as "whooping and hollering and pouring beer on your head." Paul Ray was a blues singer who pulled up stakes in Dallas and moved to Austin, bringing along his guitarist, Jimmy Vaughan. Vaughan's younger brother, Stevie Ray Vaughan, also an aspirant blues musician, would follow them a little later. Paul Ray recalled those days for Austin critic John T. Davis: "Nobody had any money, but it didn't take much. You used to be able to live on nothing. When we moved here, our rent was $45 a month. Beer was three quarts for a dollar, or you could get loaded on Boone's Farm (wine) and that was just a buck." Ray, the Vaughan brothers, and a host of other artists found Austin ideal for the incubation of their work, a haven from the conventional values so stifling in the commercial centers of Texas. With live music in cheap clubs available downtown, on the east side, and out in the country, Austin looked almost like a white middle-class refugee's version of that fertile musical melting pot of the 1920s, Dallas' seething "Deep Ellum" district.

One of the key immigrants was Willie Nelson. When his Nashville house burned to the ground at Christmastime in 1969, Willie returned to the Texas he had left in a '41 Buick nearly a decade earlier. In Bandera, a bucolic hill country town outside San Antonio, he licked the wounds Nashville had dealt him and took his road band into scores of out-of-the-way beer joints and dance halls across the state. Willie played real Texas country music, a habit that had earned him a colder reception in Nashville

than he had once hoped for. Although Music Row liked his lyrics, and didn't mind making him a wealthy songwriter, its executives found his vocal and performance talents too raw for their tastes. They heard too much eclecticism in his music, too many blues licks and jazz phrases for it rightly to be considered "country," as Nashville defined the term in the 1960s. "If a song had more than three chords in it, it wasn't commercial," complained Willie.

Back in Texas, though, Willie and the band could play what they liked. Born in 1933 in Abbott, a hamlet between Waco and Fort Worth, Nelson had learned gospel songs at his grandmother's knee; had heard blues chants in the cotton fields; had listened to Western Swing and the *Grand Ole Opry* and jazz and pop hits on the radio. He had gone to "singing cowboy" movies and learned the chords to honky-tonk songs out of the Ernest Tubb songbooks his piano-playing sister Bobbie acquired. But especially he had listened to Bob Wills. Wills' music contained a little of everything, from old-time fiddle tunes to hot jazz. (Wills, too, was a man Nashville found hard to understand.) Wills had become Willie's idol. With his brother-in-law Bud Fletcher, married to sister Bobbie, Willie also had sometimes dabbled in booking talent for nearby nightclubs. One night, the thirteen-year-old Willie had fulfilled a fantasy by hiring his hero to play a dance in neighboring Whitney. He had even managed to get on stage and play along on a song or two.

Steeped in Texas musical lore, Willie Nelson played in the little backwoods bars to kindred spirits who recognized a polka, a schottische, or a Bob Wills song when they heard one. But in Austin he saw something else: a whole new potential audience for country music, Texas country music, *his* country music. Armadillo World Headquarters, transformed in 1970 from a National Guard armory, was gaining a national reputation as a rock emporium, packing in 1,500 people on a good night. After a chat with owners Eddie Wilson and Mike Tolleson — themselves not slow to see the benefits of an expanded audience — Willie brought his band to the Armadillo in 1972. The rest, as they say, is history.

The young rockers loved Willie, and he expanded their education in country music by lining up other acts like Waylon Jennings and Tom T. Hall. The music brought together cowboys, farm boys, and other pilgrims who previously would not have been caught dead in a room with a hippie. Some nights you could have even seen the sainted Texas football coach, Darrell Royal, in the back of the hall — the rough equivalent of discovering John Wayne at a gathering of hobbits. And thus emerged the redneck-rock crossover audience. Willie consolidated it with a string of "picnics," starting with the First Annual Dripping Springs Reunion of 1972 and continuing to the Willie Nelson Fourth of July Picnics of the present day. There fans young and old come together to hear rock and country music and thank the Lord for being Texan. Through it all, to the younger generation Willie played teacher, preacher, and link with the musical past.

"The audience progressed along with the rest of us," he told Michael Bane of *Country Music* magazine. "We entered into a new field — there were young people out there who didn't know Ernest Tubb from anybody."

As Willie's presence catalyzed the diverse elements whose alliance produced the "Austin sound," hordes of others also flocked to town, attracted by the action like iron filings to a magnet. *Time* magazine called the place "the fastest-growing country-music center in the U.S." *Rolling Stone's* Chet Flippo issued dire warnings about the possibly impending industrialization of the once-sleepy hamlet. Many local observers did indeed fear a flood of record industry hucksters sweeping in from the East and West coasts, intent to package this pastoral innocence for American consumers. Others, of course, eagerly anticipated that very event. Southwestern regional music was approaching critical mass.

Joe Gracey wanted the scene to grow; he wanted Texas music to resume its rightful place in the national scheme of things. Gracey, music director at a country station in Fort Worth before coming to Austin in 1969, was program director and deejay at KOKE-FM. His playlist at KOKE sandwiched cuts by Austin bands into fare by "renegade" Nashville artists such as Waylon Jennings, Tompall Glaser, and David Allan Coe, and the new California breed of reformed rockers like the Flying Burrito Brothers.

Gracey also wrote a column called "Rock Beat" for the *Austin American-Statesman,* the town's only daily newspaper. He used his column as a pulpit from which he tirelessly preached the idea that young urban Texans ought to be more aware of their musical heritage. In 1972, Gracey heard that Dallas' public television station, Channel 13, wanted to tape some Austin bands. It looked like cultural imperialism to him. He issued a challenge to the local PBS station, KLRN Channel 9 (Austin – San Antonio).

"The Austin hippie-country bands (Greezy Wheels, Balcones Fault, and Freda and the Firedogs) will be on a Channel 13 PBS broadcast to be taped in Dallas," Gracey wrote. "Thus the good word spreads. Why didn't Austin's own public station do it first? Austin is rumbling with excitement, talent, and bands, and is about to inject some of its burgeoning culture into the national awareness. . . . The local media should be first, not the last, to hear the news."

Bill Arhos, KLRN program director, read Gracey's remarks with some sensitivity. A large, easy-going fellow of Greek ancestry, fond of fishing, pro basketball, and old pocket knives, he had come to KLRN in 1960, when he was twenty-six. Now he was casting about for a program of national significance that could originate from the Austin station. Arhos could entertain such ambitious notions, first, because he had brand-new premises and equipment. For this he could thank Robert F. Schenkkan, president and general manager of the station. Many considered Schenkkan the father of educational television at the University of Texas; the new facilities owed much to his vision and political savvy. Schenkkan, too, wanted to see important national programming come out of Austin, and he knew it would have to be more than the usual stuffy "talking heads" kind of PBS fare.

Arhos could think big, second, because the Public Broadcasting Service, the national public television network, had just instituted something called the Station Program Cooperative. The SPC, in theory at least, would make it possible for any station in the system to produce national programming, thus breaking the virtual monopoly on such programming held by New York, Boston, Los Angeles, and similar major markets. Arhos needed a subject. He had been mulling over some kind of music show for quite a while. Occasionally he kicked the idea around over breakfast with his businessman pal Howard Chalmers. And he asked Paul Bosner to think about it.

Bosner had come to KLRN from the CBS studios in New York, where he had worked as a cameraman for nineteen years. He and his crew had captured an Emmy award for their work on *Studio One,* remembered still as probably the best television dramatic series of the sixties; theirs was the first Emmy ever awarded for live camera work. But Bosner grew tired

Bill Arhos

Bruce Scafe

of repeating himself and left CBS. Now he lived in Dallas and commuted weekly to Austin to produce the national Spanish-English children's series *Carrascolendas* and other educational programs at KLRN. Still, he wanted more scope. After sampling Austin music in several popular nightclubs, he decided that a live concert program just might work. Bruce Scafe thought so, too.

Scafe had come to KLRN from WFAA-TV, an ABC network station in Dallas. Before WFAA he had been staff director at WSIU-TV, a public television station at Southern Illinois University in Carbondale. There he directed a well-received music program, *The Session,* and a ninety-minute variety program with pool immortal Minnesota Fats called *You're in Good Company.* With a degree in music as well as in radio-television-film, Scafe worked sometimes as a professional musician. He had played trumpet with the jazz bands of Maynard Ferguson and Les Elgart, among others. His empathy with the needs of other musicians, along with an obsessive determination to "get it right," had made *The Session* a success. A difficult show, it was broadcast live, with no chance for second takes or editing from tapes. The series contained seventy half-hour shows, including acts by REO Speedwagon and an obscure young singer named Billy Joel. Scafe had never heard of Willie Nelson.

Although Scafe's first musical love was jazz, he was willing to direct a music program of any kind. KLRN-TV had just moved out of its ancient cramped quarters on the university campus into the fruit of Schenkkan's labors, the new building next to "the Drag" (Guadalupe Street), the main thoroughfare in the area. The new structure was eye-catching, to say the least. Covered by an unpainted iron sheath, it rose dramatically above the rest of the "communications complex" to which it belonged. The archi-

Charlie Daniels, Paul Bosner

tect had apparently envisaged the iron oxidizing slowly in the Texas weather until the rust grew beautiful. Critics hooted and pointed at the red stains oozing down the limestone blocks on which the metal skin rested. Students, naturally, immediately dubbed the edifice "the rusty building" and went about their business. KLRN personnel, for their part, blithely ignored architects and their detractors alike. They responded instead to the potential of the huge studios and the glittering hardware housed therein. At their command stood technical equipment any commercial station might have envied. Scafe and Bosner both thought televising live concert performances would be a very good use for Studio 6A.

With Bosner and Scafe talking about a music project, and Gracey lobbing criticism from the newspaper (while his colleague Townsend Miller tirelessly touted the merits of country music in a second column), the light began to dawn on Arhos. It finally broke when he read *The Improbable Rise of Redneck Rock* by local writer Jan Reid. Reid, a native of Wichita Falls, covered the sports beat for the weekly newspaper in New Braunfels, a small German town about fifty miles from Austin — circumstances which meant a steady diet of high school athletics. He often came to Austin for relief, and there became interested in the transformation of country music he saw taking place. Published in 1974, his book was a journalist's report on a budding cultural phenomenon. Being described in print, of course, conferred a sort of legitimacy on Austin's hybrid musical issue. The scales fell from Arhos' eyes.

"You get an idea how far behind the scene I was when you realize that it existed long enough for a book to be written and published about it," he said. "It was obvious. What was the most visible cultural product of Austin? It'd be like ignoring a rhinoceros

in your bathtub." He gave Bosner and Scafe the go-ahead, and tried to round up some money.

More than anything else, the technical challenge of "translating" the spirit of a live musical event to another medium intrigued Bosner. He didn't want to capture the music itself — he didn't care whether it was country or classical or anything in between — so much as he wanted to catch the interplay between performer and audience, their mutual participation in an experience. He and Scafe worked on an idea for the set. Scafe wanted an intimate arrangement, with some of the audience surrounding and even sitting on the stage. This would make it possible for the director to cut immediately from musician to spectator and back again.

Set designer Augie Kymmel and Scafe scrounged materials for the stage and bleachers from the basement and wherever else they could find them. There were no tables or chairs on the floor. Instead, Scafe and Kymmel put down an old carpet on which people sprawled pop-festival style, sometimes thronging the floor so that the cameras could hardly move. (After each performance the set had to be struck to clear the studio for *Carrascolendas*.) Scafe and Bosner thought the studio large enough for a camera crane, too; a crane would give them unobstructed overhead shots. The station didn't have one — they are generally a luxury on the PBS circuit — but they hunted up an antique. Gradually Studio 6A took on the appearance of a small concert arena.

Vigorously attacking "glitz" and all its pomps, Bosner stressed that he wanted no professional tricks of the trade in this production — no split screens, no tricky zooms, no freezes. He wanted honesty. The only way the camera would capture the truth of the event was for all concerned to concentrate not on technique but on understanding their subject: the music and its audience. For him, student camera operators and technicians were just fine. He preferred rawness and directness to glitter and polish. Bosner described his vision in a memo:

Difficult though it may be the essence that is to be recorded on tape is that magic that floats back and forth between the musician and the audience, an energy that permeates the atmosphere. The set-design will encompass a sculptural concept, i.e., the audience and playing area will be one unit. Audience and musicians will be part of the same space. The set will contain several levels and surfaces on which audience will sit, recline, stand, move (dance). Musicians will play and sing to the audience and to each other. There will be no need to establish a visual point of view (reference) as to where the camera is — it will be everywhere seeking out relationships, audience to musicians, musicians to each other, musicians to audience. The camera will work 360 degrees around the space occupied by the audience and musicians. It is in this manner that we intend to capture the meaning, pleasure, the identification of the audience to this music.

The station's upper management did not wholly share Arhos' and Bosner's enthusiasm for the project. Nevertheless Arhos managed to nail down $13,000 in pilot money — $6,000 of which he had to return because he'd written the proposal so poorly — and got Mike Tolleson, booking agent and part owner of Armadillo World Headquarters, to book B. W. ("Buckwheat") Stevenson and Willie Nelson for two nights in November. In 1974 B. W. Stevenson, a veteran of the folk circuit in Denton and Dallas and possessor of a fat contract with RCA, was a bigger name than Willie Nelson. But word of the concert spread slowly, and by showtime B. W.'s fans had only half filled the studio. Since the set was supposed to suggest a packed house, the sparse attendance under-

cut the concept severely, despite a good performance by Stevenson.

"It looked like we gave a party and nobody came," said a rueful Arhos.

Luck improved the following night. The day brought the news that the money to pay for the pilot had been approved, and then Willie Nelson filled the house — an early indication of the drawing power that would soon catapult him into national superstardom. Since the Dripping Springs Reunion of 1972, Willie had acquired a steadily growing corps of Austin followers who would not willingly miss the magic of any of his performances, let alone a free one. These fans included young folk with noticeably long hair as well as veteran country music listeners who had loved him from the beginning. His ACL show attracted a typical Nelson audience: wonderfully diverse, enthusiastic, and celestially confident of having a great time. Willie did not disappoint them. Playing old favorites and new songs, stringing together his trademark medleys and improvising like jazz musicians, Willie and his band jacked up the energy level until the rusty building seemed to rise and levitate over the Texas campus. It was exactly what the director, producer, and program director at KLRN had hoped for. Robert Schenkkan sent them a memo. "Absolutely sensational job!" it said.

The show pleased Willie, too. Long distrustful of television's capacity to communicate good music, especially in live performance — a distrust only too well borne out by slick contemporary productions like *Don Kirschner's Rock Concert* and *Midnight Special* — Nelson had consistently refused to appear on TV. Now, hanging out in the control room watching the tapes roll, he and the band liked what they saw. Here they had room to stretch out and play their kind of music, without commercial intrusions. They offered to help any way they could. A productive partnership had begun.

To sell the series to PBS, Arhos needed a name. Maybe something like "Hill Country Rain," he thought, after Jerry Jeff Walker's song. Bruce Scafe's daughter suggested "Austin Space," because it sounded like "Lost in Space." "River City Country" was another candidate. In Washington, D.C., for a PBS meeting, Arhos went out for some air and noticed a movie marquee featuring *Macon County Line.* How about "Travis County Line"? he wondered. No, too close.

Paul Bosner, meanwhile, on every trip he made from Dallas to Austin encountered the Texas Highway Department's "Austin City Limits" sign at the north edge of town. The image gradually merged in his mind with the music he heard during his nights in the clubs. He liked the ring of it, too. "I've got the perfect title," he told Scafe. When he filmed the show's "lead-in," he started with shots of the countryside, worked toward the city — lingering on the city limits sign — then focused on the names of various local nightclubs, suggesting in this way the theme of country coming to the city. For each program, a sound track of the band's afternoon rehearsal would accompany the sequence. The closing shot would then frame the empty stage, from which the camera would dissolve to the live set as the band swung into its first number. Arhos loved the concept and he loved the title. *Austin City Limits:* yes, perfect!

Some of the station's executives, however, refused to see disseminating country music as part of the public broadcasting system's social mission. KLRN, after all, was short for K-LEARN. America seemed generally to regard commercial-free television as somehow a bit sinful, a voluptuous indulgence for which the viewer could only atone by getting educated. Certainly, from the point of view of management, asking the government for dollars to subsidize learning was easier than asking it to support a pro-gram of popular music — particularly music as . . . *unconventional* . . . as some of this stuff. Did a show purveying redneck music really befit the *dignity* of Austin's educational television station? President Schenkkan's associates in the front offices did not all think so.

"It's too provincial to sell," complained one.

"Nobody likes that shit," said another.

At this point Arhos and Bosner had little more than a one-hour pilot program and a gleam in their eyes. How *would* they sell it? Arhos took the pilot along to the second annual PBS Station Independence Project meeting, where programming for the following year's national membership drive would be discussed. Greg Harney, one of Bosner's former CBS colleagues, headed up program acquisition for the fund drive, and Arhos intended to pitch the KLRN pilot to him. It horrified him, then, to hear Harney announce to the gathered assembly that they would be trying out a one-hour country music special shot by KERA in Dallas with Willie Nelson! It turned out that Willie had indeed taped a show with KERA; but Arhos knew the Dallas studio was small and its technical facilities inferior to those of KLRN. Positive that he had the better tape, he worked on Harney until he agreed to use it instead.

In the spring 1975 national membership and fund-raising campaign, thirty-four stations, or about half the number using special programming to solicit new members, aired the Austin City Limits pilot, with encouraging results. It hit the top ten in dollars per minute, size of average pledge, and every other category station executives use to gauge financial effectiveness. This gave Arhos something to hang his hat on; and he would need good numbers as dearly as a good title if he wanted to sell a national series.

Set for Season 1

Arhos wrote a proposal for a thirteen-week progressive country music series called Austin City Limits and submitted it to the Station Program Cooperative. The SPC, however, limited screenings to ten minutes per proposal, a curtailment obviously detrimental to the show's major premise, namely, that a concert-length show amounted to a different animal entirely from a two- or three-song plug in the style of, say, *Saturday Night Live.* Wanting more than ten minutes' worth of visibility, Arhos dubbed the Nelson pilot onto twenty-two cassettes and sent them to twenty-two colleagues, with postage, mailing addresses, and directions to forward them to twenty-two additional colleagues, then another round of colleagues, then back to him. None of the cassettes ever came home.

At the SPC meeting the proposal fell distinctly short of enough votes to get it purchased and began steadily losing support. Apparently the time for country music as public television fare had not yet arrived. Arhos gave up. But then PBS decided that a program could stay in the market if it could get a consortium of five stations to support it. Still, Arhos saw no hope, until KQED-TV in San Francisco called to ask his support for one of their productions. Suddenly the full possibilities of American dealmaking thrust themselves upon him. He got the five stations ten minutes before the PBS deadline. Austin City Limits, at least for a year, would join such products of the Station Program Cooperative as *Sesame Street, Nova, Soundstage, Wall Street Week,* and *Bill Moyers' Journal* on the air waves of the nation.

Quotations not otherwise identified are from interviews (see Acknowledgments). Newspaper and magazine quotes are in some cases from clippings kept by Austin City Limits personnel; it has not always been possible to determine the dates for these.

Douglas B. Green is cited by Michael Bane, *Willie: An Unauthorized Biography of Willie Nelson* (New York: Dell, 1984), p. 173. Paul Ray is quoted by John T. Davis, "The True-Blue Soul of Stevie Ray," *Austin American-Statesman,* 16 July 1985, *Onward* magazine, pp. 19–20. Much of the information on Willie Nelson is from Bane's biography. Nelson's remark about songs with more than three chords is from John T. Davis, "The Making of Willie's Special," *Austin American-Statesman,* 18 January 1983, *Onward* magazine, pp. 10–11. *Time*'s article on Austin, "Groover's Paradise," appeared 9 September 1974, p. 70. Chet Flippo's warnings were in "Austin: The Hucksters Are Coming," *Rolling Stone,* 11 April 1974, p. 34.

FOLLOWING on the conceptual heels of the Willie Nelson pilot, the first year's series stuck close to home in its choice of music. Unable to reach an agreement with Mike Tolleson, Arhos called Joe Gracey to see if he would act as talent consultant. The call astonished Gracey — he had no idea anybody bothered to read his column — but he leaped at the chance to proselytize Texas music from an electronic forum. The acts he brought to ACL pretty much reflected the heart of his KOKE playlist: progressive country and off-beat Southwestern music.

In late summer 1975, taping began for the official 1976 programming season. If the producer and his crew of neophyte technicians felt nervous, they were also thrilled. A renaissance of Southwestern music was brewing, and they stood in precisely the right place to chronicle it. Unfortunately, not everybody in Austin shared this sense of historical importance. Some bands had difficulty filling the studio. There were days when staff members heated up the phone wires to Gracey at the radio station, asking him to plug the free tickets a little harder — prospects for the evening looked thin.

Certain technical bugs appeared, too. With little experience staging concerts, KLRN staff engineers misjudged the capacity of their equipment. During Rusty Wier and the Filler Brothers' rehearsal on the afternoon of the first taping, the monitor speakers burst into flame. Wier reputedly played hot music, but nobody had expected *this.* Hastily the station hired Dean Rabourn and his company, Spirit Sound, veterans of numerous giant pop festivals, to provide equipment for the evening. Brought in as a temporary measure, they stayed for the duration. Another problem concerned the cameras. Wier played so loud that the cameras vibrated, creating a phenomenon called "microphonics" which interfered with the picture. The show came to a halt. While the crew stuffed foam rubber padding into the cameras, Wier entertained the audience with jokes. It was getting to be a long day for him.

Most of the acts Gracey booked for ACL this first season came from the local music scene, for two reasons: They were available, and they were cheap. Gracey wanted to showcase Southwestern music to a wider audience, while KLRN executives wanted to cut costs. The Austin pool of what had come to be called progressive country musicians admirably suited both purposes.

Progressive country was actually a rather loose-fitting label that did not precisely suit all the musicians who wore it. It referred chiefly to a core of singer-songwriters who had known one another and played together for years. Many of them had started out as "folksingers" and still frequently performed solo; but when they required accompaniment, they tended to draw on the same crew of like-minded instrumentalists who lived in Austin. Thus evolved a group of accomplished musicians who dubbed themselves the Austin Interchangeable Band. They might accompany Michael Murphey, Steve Fromholz, Alvin Crow, Bobby Bridger, or Jerry Jeff Walker as the occasion arose, then go off and play in local jazz or rock pickup groups. Tomás Ramírez, for example, a brilliant saxophonist, played as a sideman with nearly everybody in town. He appeared almost a dozen times on Austin City Limits with various bands, in addition to fronting Jazzmanian Devil, his own jazz-rock group, on the show in season seven. Members of the Lost Gonzo Band had similar careers. After years of playing behind Murphey, Walker, and Bridger, they struck out on their own. They cut several records and appeared in their own right on ACL in 1978 before finally folding.

Hugh Cullen Sparks in a University of Texas doctoral dissertation — for, yes, Austin progressive country has become the stuff of Ph.D. degrees — underscores the point that these singer/songwriters were not just commercial musicians but poets and philosophers, people with a message. In any event, the music created by this Austin cadre tended more toward folk and rock than "hard" country, whether old-time or commercial. Only after Willie Nelson's influence became more pervasive and musicians such as the Interchangeable Band members began jamming on "real" country tunes after-hours did hard-core country's popularity pick up among young Austinites.

If progressive country dominated ACL's maiden season, important exceptions occurred also. In keeping with his private educational mission, Gracey booked Clifton Chenier and Flaco Jiménez, both consummate accordion artists rarely heard outside the Southwest. Chenier reigned as Louisiana's King of Zydeco. Zydeco, a combination of rhythm and blues and string-band music, flourished along the Gulf Coast where Southeast Texas meets Southwest Louisiana. Clifton had regularly kept Austin fans jumping all night, ever since Carlyn Majewski of Soap Creek Saloon first imported him. Flaco had grown up on San Antonio's west side, the son of *conjunto* pioneer Santiago Jiménez. Now he played his red-hot music for *tejano* audiences throughout South Texas. No one who heard either Flaco

or Clifton in live performance would be likely to forget the experience. Still, although their musical styles were integral to Texas, they hardly belonged to the popular mainstream. Gracey could only cross his fingers and hope for the best.

Surely from a historical standpoint the most important show of the first season had to be the reunion of the original Texas Playboys. Spanning a good four decades, Bob Wills and His Texas Playboys had become synonymous with the music they made famous, Western Swing. Scores of musicians had passed through Wills' band during that time, but the original Playboys — the ones he started out with in the thirties — had mostly fallen away in 1943 when Wills went into the Army. By 1960 Western Swing had mainly petered out; Wills continued to play with smaller and smaller bands, finally ending as a solo act. His massive stroke in 1969 signaled the end of even that. It had long been his dream to reunite with the pre-war Playboys, some of whom he hadn't seen for thirty years, for one last time.

One-time Playboys were now pumping gas, driving trucks, and working in warehouses. Opportunities to play were rare. Merle Haggard recruited a few of the original Playboys for his 1971 album, *Tribute to the Best Damn Fiddle Player in the World (or, My Personal Salute to Bob Wills)*. In 1972 the band regrouped to do a benefit for Wills in Fort Worth. Wills occupied a wheelchair, but managed to join in on a chorus or two. Out of that came the idea to record a final album, and so in 1973 the Playboys entered a Dallas studio. The album was originally to be titled *Homecoming*. Bob Wills attended the first day, but that evening suffered another stroke, from which he did not recover. The Playboys finished the recording session on the second day, and changed the album's name to *For the Last Time*. Wills died in 1975. The Austin City Limits con-

Clifton Chenier

cert would be the first appearance of the original Texas Playboys since the 1973 recording session, and only the second time that many of them had played together in nearly forty years.

Ironically, the show was in some respects an accident. Bob Wills' widow, Betty, owned the rights to the "Texas Playboys" name, and she wanted no reunions after Bob's death. Gracey did not know this when he called as many of the old Playboys as he could track down and lined them up for the performance; later he discovered the problem. By then, luckily, the wheels had begun to turn. Betty Wills graciously consented to the Playboys' appearance and decided to attend the show.

Gracey's success at securing the musicians led to another interesting problem: While he had eleven Playboys signed on for the show, he had money to pay only five. What to do? Bobby Earl Smith, who with Marcia Ball had started Freda and the Firedogs and was now manager and bass player for Alvin Crow and the Pleasant Valley Boys, had become good friends with Gracey. Smith remembers sitting at home one morning, idly listening to Gracey's show, when he heard his name issue from the radio: "Bobby Earl! Call me quick!" He did, but Gracey would only say, "Come down to the station." There he told Smith the problem. Smith's response was to head directly to the Broken Spoke, a venerable Austin dance hall, whose manager happily agreed to book the Texas Playboys on short notice. Tickets went on sale for $5.00 — a substantial price in those days — and sold out, and that's how the Playboys made expenses. The arrangement recalled the band's fast and loose touring days of the thirties. (Actually, many of ACL's early guests would try to book gigs in Austin to supplement the show's meager wages.)

Bob Wills, the "King of Western Swing" in Waylon Jennings' paean,

had fronted the most famous and influential band to come out of Texas. The Texas parents and grandparents of the Alvin Crow generation had all danced to Bob Wills, sung along with his songs on the radio, and absorbed his vocal mannerisms, such as his famous falsetto *ah-hah,* into their everyday discourse. Yet their children, weaned on the rockabilly of Buddy Holly and Elvis Presley and Carl Perkins, remained largely ignorant of Bob Wills and the Playboys. They didn't know that his music encompassed a lot more than the old warhorse "San Antonio Rose," or that Wills was an innovator whose jazz-fired country music had taken the nation by storm before they were born.

Of course, western swing didn't spring full-blown from Bob Wills' head. But Wills and Milton Brown were the real pioneers. Born into a family of fiddlers, Wills traveled with a medicine show and did blackface comedy routines in small Texas towns during the twenties. Then he met Milton Brown, whose vocal style impressed him mightily. Brown joined Wills and guitarist Herman Arnspiger to form the original Light Crust Doughboys in 1931, advertising flour to Depression-strapped farmers over radio station KFJZ in Fort Worth. The Doughboys would last half a century, and many of the Dallas–Fort Worth area's best musicians would pass through the band; but both Brown and Wills had left to start their own groups by 1933.

Milton Brown and His Musical Brownies were the seedbed of "country jazz." Brown's band sounded like a breathless sort of countrified pop, but eventually became more jazz-oriented. Fred Calhoun, called "Papa" because of his affinity with Earl "Fatha" Hines, said that, so far as he knew, when he joined Brown for a guest set at the Crystal Springs Club in Fort Worth, it was the first time a piano had ever played with a country fiddle band. The Brownies became the hottest band in Fort Worth, but after Milton Brown's death in a car wreck in 1936, the heart went out of the organization.

By the time of World War II, Bob Wills and the Texas Playboys had become identified with Western Swing, the label that finally stuck to the hybrid they and Milton Brown had pioneered. The music spoke to the needs of a generation of Texans — indeed, of Americans, on the move. It contained the comfortable truths they had grown up with, but it also had a rhythm and sophistication — a *swing* — more in keeping with the beat of their lives. In the dance halls and honkytonks they could meet and flirt and socialize to its pleasant pulse, and at home it kept them company on the radio. Western Swing burgeoned into a national phenomenon. In 1968, although Wills and the Playboys had never thought of themselves as playing "country music" — "It wasn't up to our level" — Nashville honored Bob by inducting him into the Country Music Hall of Fame.

Asleep at the Wheel, a young group of bona fide Bob Wills disciples, shared the Austin City Limits program with the Playboys. Led by Ray Benson, they had originated in California, playing bars up and down the state. (Bob Wills himself had gone to California in 1943; he often played to tens of thousands at the Venice Pier Ballroom. Western Swing had taken root in the Golden State and, like many things Californian, had waxed glossier and smoother than its Texas antecedent until it too declined.) In 1973 Asleep at the Wheel had arrived in Austin to play Antone's, an outstanding local blues club; the band felt so much at home they decided to stay. They succeeded in bringing Western Swing back to the country charts, and now the chance to play with the Texas Playboys meant another dream come true. (Their 1974 album, *Fathers and Sons*, contained

two records: one held their own music; the second was simply a reissue of early Bob Wills songs.) For their part, the Playboys appreciated the admiration and musical support of these talented youngsters.

The Playboys' show surpassed everyone's expectations, including those of Betty Wills. Recognition rippled through the youthful audience as many of them filled a gap in their musical background. "I finally found out where 'Take it away, Leon' came from," exclaimed a smooth-faced stu-

Texas Playboys

dent when steel guitarist Leon McAuliffe kicked off his steel guitar break to Wills' familiar cry, uttered here by Keith Coleman. A generation of Texas farm boys had been exhorted by their fathers to "Take it away, Leon" in one context or another, while they wondered to themselves just who the hell Leon was, anyway. Now a lucky few of them found out.

The new PBS series could hardly have chosen more auspicious material for its television debut. By the end of the taping, tears streamed down the faces of musicians, cameramen, and audience alike. An emotional Leon McAuliffe, speaking for the band, told the audience, "I can't tell you how good you make a bunch of old men, a few middle-aged men, and one young man feel." The ACL staff knew then that they could capture history. The soundtrack of the ACL program was released as a double album on Delta Records, and the Country Music Association requested a copy of the videotape for its Hall of Fame archives in Nashville. The Playboys themselves went on to a second career that ten years later still had them performing twenty or thirty times a year.

When the tenth season of Austin City Limits rolled around, coinciding with the Texas Playboys' fiftieth anniversary as performers, it seemed only appropriate to have them back again. This time they played on Congress Avenue on an outdoor stage in front of the state capitol. ("Reminds me of the street broadcasts we used to do back in the thirties," said Eldon Shamblin.) The streets were thronged, and for this show the Austin City Limits trademark view of the Austin skyline was not a studio set, but the real thing.

Hugh Cullen Sparks' dissertation is "Stylistic Developments and Compositional Processes of Selected Solo Singers/Songwriters in Austin, Texas" (University of Texas at Austin, 1984).

THE FIRST ACL SEASON presented thirteen one-hour programs. Eight of these devoted themselves to one band only; the rest consisted of two thirty-minute segments, each with a different band. Each band's show was boiled down from roughly ninety minutes of videotape. By today's standards, the editing process was crude. It consisted simply of splicing songs together, smoothing transitions between them, and synchronizing the video with the audio. It sounds easier than it was.

To begin with, the studio owned a limited number of the machines required for editing tape, and other programs used them during regular broadcast hours. This meant that Scafe and his crew could not begin work until midnight, when the station signed off. They left at six, when the daily broadcast began. It usually took all night to get thirty minutes of finished tape. Since everyone working on Austin City Limits also held a day job at the station, there was little time left for sleeping. Arhos sometimes came to the work sessions and slept on the floor. Scafe remembers leaving the studio early one morning, and stopping his car for a blinking red light. The next thing he knew, a policeman was informing him that he'd been stationary for ten minutes, and how much longer did he think it would take for the light to turn green?

The system was primitive. The editors could not re-mix the sound, for instance. What went on the air was essentially an edited version of the "live" or "rough" mix captured by audio engineer David Hough, nothing more. The studio employed a "double system," meaning that different machines recorded the sound and the visuals. Matching up audio and video constituted the main job of editing. Since a "time-coding" system did not yet exist, the crew had to make the synch manually. They used two editing machines, so one requirement was a technician with long arms. He would roll one machine, then the other; Scafe would stand back, and when video and sound seemed to emanate from one source instead of two,

he would say "You're in synch." The technician would punch the "Edit" button, and sight and sound would mesh, or so everyone hoped. But if a frame slipped, as often happened, or something else was off, they retreated directly to square one, with maybe an hour lost.

They also had to make purely video editing decisions. Paul Bosner liked wide shots; he wanted to see the audience playing its part in the "concert experience." Scafe basically agreed; television had a natural tendency to bore people with too many close-ups, he believed. But he was, after all, a musician. He liked counterpoint. He sought to achieve a correspondence between musical values and video images. He might, for example, cut to a "relief shot" of the crowd, say, when the music was relatively relaxed. Then when an intense lyric or a complex run built the tension again, he would go in tight with the camera. "For me," he said, "a music program benefits when the visual element — its own 'phrasing,' its highs and lows — can be music, too. The cameraman's temptation is always to focus on the person who's singing or soloing. But as a musician, I'm not always interested in that. I like to see the performer putting the whole thing to-

**SEASON 1
1976**

101 Asleep at the Wheel
     The Texas Playboys
102 Rusty Wier
103 Clifton Chenier
     Townes Van Zandt
104 Augie Meyers
     Flaco Jimenez
105 Doug Sahm
106 Alvin Crow
107 Steve Fromholz
108 B. W. Stevenson
     Bobby Bridger
109 Greezy Wheels
     Wheatfield
110 Balcones Fault
111 Marcia Ball
112 The Charlie Daniels
     Band
113 Jerry Jeff Walker

gether." The differences in point of view between producer and director were perhaps subtle but frequently took time to resolve. At these junctures David Hough would try to catch up on his sleep.

Hough had decisions of his own to make, regarding the sound quality of the audio track. He too was a jazz musician; he played drums. Sometimes at parties he would jam with Scafe. His musicianship no doubt contributed to his passion for audio quality. "David's rough mixes are better than most engineers' final mixes," Scafe would say. Among other things, he had to think about "perspective," that is, the position from which the audience might hear the music: up close, where the instruments would sound bright and distinct, or further back, where they would blend into one sound. When the band started playing, Hough might have over a score of onstage microphone sources to mix into his multitrack recorder. It gave him an adrenalin rush, in these early days, knowing that there would be no re-mix, that he had to get it all the first time. The situation recalled sound recording conditions of the 1930s — the decade of Bob Wills' and Milton Brown's first sides — before the invention of tape machines, when engineers etched a performance directly on the master disk, with no chance to correct mistakes by "getting it in the mix." More than one musician, Willie Nelson among them, has felt that that directness contributed an immediacy and excitement which disappeared when more sophisticated recording techniques came into being.

Hough agreed that television is a close-up medium and tried to catch the feel of such a perspective. Wishing to avoid favoritism to his own instrument, the drums, he nevertheless boosted the bass end to compensate for the low-frequency inadequacies of the three-inch television speaker, whose designers had the human voice

rather than music in mind. (Freedom from the tyranny of bad speakers would finally come with the inception of the FM radio "simulcast," which did for realistic concert sound what Henry Ford did for the automobile.)

Hough's methods evidently worked. When Chet Atkins decided to play ACL in its third year, he expressed concern about the sound mix, an understandable interest in a consummate instrumentalist and former head of RCA's Nashville recording studios. After hearing Hough's work, however, Atkins conferred his imprimatur and left the decisions entirely up to the KLRN audio room.

A rawness and immediacy, almost an urgency, characterized the first season's thirteen programs. For Scafe and his crew it was a labor of love. The schedule hurt: taping a show one night, spending the next two or three nights editing, then preparing for the next performance, all the while handling daytime duties at KLRN. More often than not, Scafe got home just in time to see his kids off to school. There was no overtime pay, and salaries in public television weren't much to write home about anyway. Yet the production team felt a commitment to the project that bordered on obsession.

Things had to be "right" whatever the cost, as in, for instance, the case of Clifton Chenier's crown. As King of Zydeco, Clifton liked to don a glittering rhinestone-and-purple velvet headpiece during his performance. The trouble was that he also doffed it as the mood took him, whether in the midst of a song or not. This practice led to interesting problems of continuity when it came to editing the tape. Scafe and Bosner worked on that one for hours, debating furiously whether anyone's grandmother in Ohio would notice the peregrinations of the crown from shot to shot.

Most of the videotape editing consisted of selecting songs and creating

transitions, rather than editing within a song. But in the second season a notable exception occurred. A show by the Earl Scruggs Revue gave rise to it. The band had played a hot number, "Bugle Call Rag," in which the energy and rapport between Scruggs and his sidemen — his sons — were outstanding. The only problem was that Earl, tired because he was recuperating from an accident, kept getting his fingers tangled in his banjo strings. He got the instrumental chorus break right only once. Eager to save the song, Scafe spliced the correct licks into the tape each time the chorus came around, meanwhile cutting the video away from Earl's fingers. When Scruggs later saw the show on television, he remarked that "Bugle Call Rag" didn't seem as bad as he remembered it. He thought the audio was good enough for a record, in fact. Eventually the Scruggs soundtrack went to Nashville and became an album called *Live! From Austin City Limits.*

Except for the original Texas Playboys, every act that taped the show the first year called Austin home or played there regularly. Even the Playboys, for that matter, had played Austin clubs at one or another point in their career. ACL's eclectic mix of talent reflected the local music scene's range. Progressive country acts predominated, with Rusty Wier, Steve Fromholz, Jerry Jeff Walker, and Charlie Daniels each receiving an hour show. B. W. Stevenson and Bobby Bridger, with the Lost Gonzo Band, had half-hour segments. Alvin Crow and Marcia Ball represented neo-traditional country music, or "gut country" as some among the younger generation called it. (Alvin Crow's repertoire featured songs by Milton Brown and Bob Wills, and his steel player, Herb Steiner, who played sometimes with Michael Murphey and Marcia Ball as well, often sounded eerily like Brown's pioneer steel guitarist, Bob Dunn.) Doug Sahm's improbable San Antonio blend of country, rock, and chicano music filled an hour of air time, as did Flaco Jiménez and his *conjunto* band, with a young Ry Cooder sitting in.

Clifton Chenier, accustomed to electrifying Austin club-goers with his Louisiana zydeco band, occupied a half-hour slot back-to-back with Townes Van Zandt, an Austin folkie songwriter whose "Pancho and Lefty," later to be recorded by Willie Nelson and Merle Haggard, was already launched toward immortality. A brace of regional bands, Greezy Wheels from Austin and Wheatfield from Houston, aired together. Another relatively unknown Austin group, Balcones Fault, received an hour of broadcast time. Balcones Fault featured a lot of horns and a big sound; though heavily rock-flavored, their arrangements recalled popular music of the forties and even vaudeville. Very popular in Austin, the band nevertheless hardly fit the mold of "progressive country." Soon after their television debut, they departed for the West Coast to make it big, as so many Austin bands had done in the sixties, and disappeared, as so many Austin bands had also done. Greezy Wheels and Wheatfield soon dissolved too.

Given the normal mortality rate of young bands, however, the batting average stands up pretty well. Very few of the eighteen bands aired during that first season were then well known outside the region. That fifteen of those have stayed alive professionally, most of them indeed flourishing, underscores the quality of the Austin musical environment that helped nourish them. But while nearly all the musicians had a strong regional following, nobody knew how Southwestern music would go over nationally. Joe Gracey, of course, believed in it, and he handled the booking. He wanted national exposure for progressive country, which he thought was the salvation of the fu-

ture. But what about "ethnic" acts like Flaco and Clifton? Would they work?

The show unmistakably aided the careers of most of the Austin bands that played it. Bobby Earl Smith, as Alvin Crow's manager, especially appreciated ACL's potential. Crow and the Pleasant Valley Boys, like a great many bands, were trying to break out of the dance hall circuit into the "showcase clubs," where they could attract media attention as a step to record contracts and expanded bookings. Austin City Limits produced exactly the effect of a showcase club. The band's appearance on television, coupled with a release on an independent record label about the same time, soon led to a contract with a major record label and then to a date at New York's Carnegie Hall. Crow got his records played on KVOO and WBAP, the radio stations of his Western Swing idols. As far as Crow and his manager were concerned, ACL was a godsend to Austin music. And as for Flaco, it turned out that, of the flood of letters received by KLRN about the show, his program inspired the greatest number. Most of them requested information on how to get his records.

All was not sweetness and light, of course. A few musicians resented the way ACL portrayed them. Although Bosner appreciated the local music scene, he could not help but stay to some degree an outsider. While he therefore possessed an outsider's objectivity, he also lacked intimate familiarity with Austin's musical evolution. This led to occasional misunderstandings, as in the case of Greezy Wheels, a vintage Austin country-rock band featuring Mary Egan's fiddling and Cleve Hattersley's vocals. Band members complained that the edited tape of their session — twenty-two minutes boiled down from ninety — distorted their image. It overemphasized "country" tunes, in their opinion, at the expense of the wilder rock material that had brought them fame. With their first album just out and careers at the make-or-break point, they worried about bad publicity. The ACL staff offered to re-edit their videotape for reruns, but felt that the real fault belonged to Greezy Wheels. Their performance had just been flat, the staff said, hardly air-worthy at all.

More serious rumblings surfaced from the local music community about the choice of artists. What exactly did the Austin City Limits title mean in terms of who appeared on the show? Charlie Daniels, for example, didn't live in Austin. Nor, for that matter, did Clifton Chenier, although he was closer, to be sure. Why name the show for Austin if you were going to bring in people from Tennessee and Louisiana? Especially if you were going to leave out local figure-heads like yodeler Kenneth Thread-gill, long-time patron of Austin folk music who had learned from Jimmie Rodgers and who had encouraged generations of Austin singers, including rock superstar Janis Joplin? Threadgill performed regularly with guitarist Bill Neely, and purer old-time country music could not be found. Perhaps such performers weren't deemed sufficiently commercial; but wasn't the major premise of the "Austin sound" precisely its anticommercialism? In the perennial battle of art versus commerce, the difference between public television and network television seemed less than clear to many musicians.

Another problem concerned censorship, although the management at KLRN would have preferred a more delicate term. For instance, some nervous discussion centered on Rusty Wier's tape, which contained his "I Heard You Been Layin' My Old Lady," not a dainty song at all. Should it be cut? The song remained, but it did indeed inspire some angry responses from participating PBS stations, whose viewers called it "filthy,

obscene, obnoxious, offensive, and repugnant." What would they have said had they seen Kinky Friedman's show?

Although PBS aired eighteen video-tapes that first season, ACL had actually shot nineteen. The one left in the can belonged to Kinky Friedman and the Texas Jewboys. Friedman had grown up in Austin, graduated from the University of Texas, served in the Peace Corps, and had pushed his music in Los Angeles and Nashville. Tompall Glaser produced an album for him, distributed by Vanguard. The Jewboys sounded polished, professional, and commercial when they wanted to, as much Nashville as Austin. The only real difference between their product and standard country-and-western radio fare lay in the lyrics. Over the most conventional accompaniment, Kinky could deliver lyrics to fry a jaded rocker's brain cells. Satirizing Mom, apple pie, and other cherished dreams of the middle class was not enough for Friedman; he had to put the Holocaust in a song ("Ride 'em Jewboy"), attack women's liberation ("Get Your Biscuits in the Oven [and Your Buns in the Bed]"), and even bring up the taboo topic of mass murder — in Texas, at UT no less, in "The Ballad of Charles Whitman" (Whitman had slain sixteen persons with sniper fire from the University of Texas tower in 1966). Kinky's loyalties sided with real country music. "The Eagles live on the charts," he once said. "But George Jones, Lefty Frizzell, and Hank Williams live in the heart." A poet, Kinky attracted to his performances literary types such as Allen Ginsberg, Bob Dylan, and Ken Kesey.

Though not really a member of the "progressive country club" — in fact he acted rather hostile to it — Kinky and the Jewboys often played Austin. ACL invited them to do the show. The taping went well, but difficulties arose when PBS network executives viewed the finished product. Many of them felt it crossed the nebulous line of "community standards." They would send it to participating stations, but only with a "flag" to signify possibly objectionable content. KLRN's management split on Kinky's acceptability, but agreed that a flag might jeopardize continuing sales of the series. They consented to hold back the videotape. The *Daily Texan,* the campus newspaper, picked up the story, as did the *Austin Sun,* a counterculture weekly, making it into a minor cause célèbre; but PBS did not yield, even when KLRN eventually offered them the show free.

The *Texan* quoted Howard Chalmers, by then Director of Development at KLRN. "Management felt that as many as half of the 114 stations that bought the series through the Public Broadcasting System would not be able to air the Friedman segment," said Chalmers, because of its "questionable taste." President and General Manager Robert Schenkkan said he was personally offended by the decision. However, conceding that Friedman was "quite a serious young man," he added that he was also "just beyond audience acceptance." Friedman himself called the decision "neanderthal." He didn't consider the show obscene. In fact, declared Kinky, "We went out of our way to clean up the act."

Nonetheless, the tape remained in the vaults, a high-energy mixture of vaudeville, medicine show, and musical satire. A decade later, current ACL producer Terry Lickona would characterize the squelch decision as classic overreaction: "I think it would have been a killer show, and probably would have gotten a terrific response — maybe some of it negative, but I think it's good to jolt people every now and then. You don't want to homogenize your show to the extent that it's not going to offend anybody, because then it's not going to stimulate anybody either." His statement is a barometer of the security

that subsequent years of success have conferred on Austin City Limits. Yet even in these more comfortable times, performers as flamboyant as superoutlaw David Allan Coe tend to tone down their acts when they get in front of the cameras.

The thirteen programs that went on the air in 1976 were greeted enthusiastically across the country. Congratulatory letters and well-wishing telegrams poured in. Arhos felt gratified; the idea he and Bosner and Scafe had hatched had proved successful. Now all he had to do was sell the series to PBS for a second season.

Kinky Friedman on the Eagles vs. George Jones et al. is quoted in "People," *Country Music,* May/June 1985, p. 21. Friedman on the withholding of his ACL show is from a 1976 interview with Martha McKenzie as is the quotation from Robert Schenkkan.

ALL THE HARD work and dedication attracted attention. Along with a growing audience, ACL in its second year would garner the Chicago Film Festival Award for Best Television Network Series. One program — no. 202, featuring Gove Scrivenor on one segment and the Amazing Rhythm Aces on the other — would also be nominated for an Emmy. National recording musicians would begin to notice the show's high quality and sense potential for their careers. In view of such promise, clearly apparent in hindsight, it may seem strange that Austin City Limits almost failed to see the light of a second season. Arhos fought to keep it afloat, but budget cuts reduced the number of shows from thirteen to ten. Paul Bosner left for England to produce Shakespeare for the BBC. Arhos became producer and Howard Chalmers executive producer.

During the off-season some internal skirmishing arose between the KLRN engineering and the ACL production staffs over Dean Rabourn and Spirit Sound. Engineering wanted to re-take control of the studio sound system. But a production memo noted that the studio sound meant much to the desired "nightclub effect." In contrast to the station's engineering department, whose members mostly came from an earlier television era during which attention to audio ran well behind attention to video, Rabourn's crew believed firmly in the credo of modern concert production: Thou shalt be faithful to a musician's unique sound. (One incident in the first season had particularly aroused Scafe's ire against the engineers. One of them had for some reason left the cymbals out of Clifton Chenier's final audio mix, perhaps because he didn't like them. To preserve compatibility between video and sound tracks, Scafe was forced to re-edit the tape and take out the cymbal shots.) Finally, after a war of memos and hallway conversations, station management decided to renew Spirit Sound's contract. The production staff sighed in relief.

The camera crane also became a permanent part of the show, even though Bosner had originally objected to this particular one as too big. Designed for movies, not for TV, the crane exuded the smell of history. There were only four of its kind made. It came from the MGM back lot, where it had lain abandoned for years after being used, supposedly, to shoot *The Wizard of Oz.* Bosner supervised renovations. The crane required a six-person crew, but proved perfect for circling behind the bleachers in the huge studio. Perched at the end of its arm, an operator had access to uninterrupted wide shots of band and audience all night long. And indeed, the program now depends on the crane camera for a "back-up tape" of every performance.

Arhos managed to sell a second season to the network, but not without twisting arms and cutting deals. Country music, even "modern" country music, didn't exactly top the wish list for most station executives around the nation. Public television, after all, had traditionally aligned itself with "high culture" — Shakespeare, literary drama, serious documentaries, and the like — and bore a certain disdain toward the more popular entertainment forms. When Spiro Agnew leveled his notorious blast at the "effete snobs" of the Eastern media es-

SEASON 2 1977

201 Tracey Nelson / Willie Nelson
202 Gove / Amazing Rhythm Aces
203 Earl Scruggs Revue
204 Rusty Wier / Jimmy Buffett
205 Delbert McClinton / Gatemouth Brown
206 Denim / Firefall
207 Steve Fromholz / Guy Clark
208 Kiwi / The Dirt Band
209 Alex Harvey / Larry Gatlin
210 Willis Alan Ramsey / Roy Buchanan

tablishment, he meant PBS dignitaries as much as anyone. Howard Chalmers, who as public relations chief had the job of generating good publicity for ACL, once commented, "Public television people are the only ones I know who can look down their noses at millionaires." Pity a Texas boy trying to peddle redneck music to these nattering nabobs!

Many station managers complained that an hour of a country act was more than sufficient (The change in format to half-hour sets came partially as a response to this complaint, as well as recognition that holding the interest of a TV audience for an hour is a difficult thing.) Furthermore, ACL often aired at fairly awkward times, particularly in the North and the West, taking a back seat to Jacques Cousteau, the Boston Pops, and other hardy perennials. Such positioning did little for audience growth. That the series was renewed for a second year may be seen as a tribute to the dogged loyalty of music fans who followed it to the obscurest corners of program schedules.

Finally the dust settled, however, and the season kicked off with Willie Nelson. Willie, who seemed on the way to becoming patron saint of the series, elected to showcase his landmark album, *The Red-Headed Stranger.* Some writers consider it the opening salvo in the country music "outlaw movement." Released by Columbia Records in 1975, the record is what the trade calls a "concept album," meaning that the songs all relate to a central theme. Concept albums did not appear often in the country music field; in fact, Willie's *Yesterday's Wine* (1971 on RCA) had been the first. *Red-Headed Stranger* tells the story of an enigmatic figure who powerfully evokes the cowboy myth. He suffers betrayal by his beloved, kills both her lover and her in revenge, and after great suffering wins a new love. The music is spare, economical, minimally produced, and flavored heavily with country gospel.

Willie recorded the album not in Nashville or New York, but at Autumn Sound Studios in Garland, Texas, and not with studio musicians but with his road band. In the studio, Willie insisted that the band be set up as if they were on stage. He wanted to capture the feel of a live performance, and so wanted the band to be able to see and hear one another. This was a throwback to "primitive" 1930s recording techniques. In most modern recording sessions the musicians are closeted in isolation booths where, listening over headsets to the rest of the band or even pre-recorded tracks, they add their own sound to the mix. Fred "Papa" Calhoun, Milton Brown's pianist, recalled the time a studio engineer separated the Musical Brownies for recording purposes. The band felt that musical interest was being sacrificed to technical improvement, and after that voted down the engineers. Echoing Calhoun, Willie Nelson told Jan Reid: "The thing about Nashville is that those session musicians are so good that it sounds like manufactured music. There's no feeling to it at all. . . . the trouble with them is that they're too perfect." At Autumn Sound, after the recording session, the engineers invited Willie to help mix the tape — the first time in his recording career anyone had asked.

Columbia Records executives were not universally happy with the distinctly non-Nashville product Willie handed them, but they released it anyway. To their considerable surprise, it became the company's first platinum country music album (meaning it sold a million copies). One of its cuts, "Blue Eyes Crying in the Rain," crossed over to the pop charts to become Willie's first Number One hit. ("Blue Eyes" was written by Hank Williams' songwriting mentor, Fred Rose, the Rose in Acuff-Rose Publications, the country music publishing company that dominated Nashville in the forties and fifties.)

Howard Chalmers, executive producer of Season 2

Rolling Stone magazine announced that the appearance of *The Red-Headed Stranger* called for a "redefinition of the term 'country music.'" In any case, it made a dramatic impact on Nashville. Willie Nelson suddenly found himself not an exile but a hero. The Country Music Association conferred awards, which he graciously accepted in blue jeans and bandana, and President Jimmy Carter invited him to lunch. Casting about for a catch-phrase to describe the "new" music — actually a throwback to the country styles of Bob Wills and Jimmie Rodgers, crossed with rockabilly — the Nashville circuit came up with the term "outlaw music." Most observers give Hazel Smith of the Glaser Brothers' studio credit for publicizing the tag. It carried the marketable connotations of revolution and cowboyhood simultaneously, and caught on like wildfire. Dave Hickey, in a January 1974 *Country Music* magazine story titled "In Defense of the Telecaster Cowboy Outlaws," remarked that the "outlaws" were "the only folks in Nashville who will walk into a room where there's a guitar and a *Wall Street Journal* and pick up the guitar."

RCA Records, seeing how the wind blew, issued an album called *Wanted! The Outlaws,* featuring Waylon Jennings, Willie, Tompall Glaser, and Waylon's wife, Jessi Colter (whose "I'm Not Lisa" was a staple of many *rock* FM stations). Though not a terrific album — it consisted mainly of outtakes and cuts from earlier records — *The Outlaws* sold like crazy. The company prudently followed it with *Waylon and Willie,* which contained "Luckenbach, Texas (Back to the Basics of Love)," a homily to the laid-back life. If Nashville couldn't beat the Austin sound, it would join it.

Back in Austin, Willie and company videotaped *The Red-Headed Stranger* as they had recorded it, together onstage. (Because Willie had shaved his beard the day of the taping, a studio security guard failed to recognize him and barred his entrance. Fortunately he persisted instead of going back home.) After the show the staff invited the band to the video control room again to sit around and make suggestions on the mixing. Such practice might be revolutionary in Nashville, but it was only standard practice on Austin City Limits.

By the time the videotape ran on PBS in spring 1977, *The Red-Headed Stranger* had dropped off the *Billboard* charts; after the broadcast it came back on for forty-eight more weeks. That's when Bill Arhos began to suspect that his favorite television show was not without power of its own. *Stranger* aired with a concert by Tracey Nelson, rhythm and blues band Mother Earth's powerhouse lead vocalist. The two Nelsons were unrelated, except musically, although they once made the charts with a duet called "Love Is Cold as Ashes (After the Fire Is Gone)."

Craig Hillis of Moon Hill Management, the booking agency for many of Austin's progressive country musicians, served as talent consultant for the second season. A musician himself, Hillis was a charter member of the Austin Interchangeable Band. He did much to educate the ACL staff on the distinction between mainstream and "outlaw" country music. Although the line-up continued to emphasize the exciting brand of music occurring in Austin, management determined to reach out for "national" talent as well. To station executives, national meant Nashville. To Hillis, Nashville meant the emerging "new wave" of musicians, a younger generation who were beginning to respond to the innovations emanating from Austin with a leaner, cleaner sound and more realistic lyrics.

Hence, in addition to Willie and Tracey Nelson, the Amazing Rhythm Aces, the Earl Scruggs Revue, and Alex Harvey, author of "Delta Dawn" (Tanya Tucker's first hit), all played

ACL. Larry Gatlin, a Texas native gone to Nashville, made his national television debut. Delbert McClinton and Gatemouth Brown presented their respective brands of deep-rooted Texas rhythm and blues; neither of them could be considered "progressive country" by any reasonable definition. Delbert's show came before he achieved national popularity. His Austin fans, used to catching him in his more natural honky-tonk milieu, failed to turn out in big numbers for the taping. The cameramen found they had to "shoot around" large empty spaces, which Selby tried to mask by creative lighting.

Rusty Wier and Steve Fromholz returned. Willis Alan Ramsey, whose soft blues-based ballads such as "Muskrat Candlelight" sounded even better in his rare concert appearances than on record, taped a show. Ramsey consciously tried to make a regional rather than a national music. "Bring back Texas color," he said. "Bring back all those differences between Texas and New York, Texas and Nebraska." Guy Clark, perhaps the best of the young songwriters, made his television debut on ACL. Clark, author of "L.A. Freeway," "Desperadoes Waiting for a Train," and an immortal train song called "Texas 1947," brought a rare brand of musical integrity to the show. His "Texas 1947" and Fromholz's "Texas Trilogy" undoubtedly remain the most quintessentially Texan country songs to date.

Roy Buchanan, guitar genius from Washington, D.C., appeared, as did the Dirt Band, having dropped their "Nitty Gritty" for the time being. So did Jimmy Buffett. There were also several young and hopeful bands whose careers would not last as long as that of their host. Except for the Scruggs Revue, which received a full hour in deference to Earl's seminal influence on country music, the performers all appeared in thirty-minute shows linked in pairs to make up the Austin City Limits hour.

The policy of combining two concerts into one television program rendered the old voice-over sound check on the lead-in sequence a bit awkward. So Bruce Scafe pulled a song out of the first season's concluding show to accompany those landscape and nightclub shots. That show featured Jerry Jeff Walker and the Lost Gonzo Band; the song Scafe chose was "London Homesick Blues" by Gary P. Nunn. Nunn had written it while touring England with Jerry Jeff, and it poignantly evoked the longing of a musician on the road for a special hometown:

I want to go home with the Armadillo,
Country music from Amarillo and
Abilene,
The friendliest people and the purtiest
women
You've ever seen.

The song seemed custom-made for Austin City Limits; it was destined to become the series theme song.

Although no one quite understood why, the show generated a special appeal. Perhaps country music possessed an honesty that television audiences in the Watergate-jaded seventies found bracing. Especially if they had formed their notions of "country" from *Hee Haw* or *The Beverly Hillbillies,* ACL must have felt like a fresh breeze. Without script, score, or choreography, here were musicians playing, people listening, and everybody having a good time as if it were the most natural thing in the world.

"Being natural" is, of course, the sine qua non of real country music, as everyone from Roy Acuff to Willie Nelson has known. Hank Williams, analyzing country music's success in his own day, put it succinctly: "It can be explained in just one word: sincerity. When a hillbilly sings a crazy song, he feels crazy. When he sings, 'I Laid My Mother Away,' he sees her a-laying right there in the coffin. He sings more sincere than most entertainers because the hillbilly was raised rougher than most entertainers. You got to know a lot about hard work. You got to have smelt a lot of mule manure before you can sing like a hillbilly. The people who has been raised something like the way the hillbilly has knows what he is singing about and appreciates it." This was printed in 1953.

But if the contents of Austin City Limits spoke to a middlebrow audience weary of too much blandness and too little grit, the series appealed in other ways too. Technically, it overshadowed its competition. Los Angeles-based commercial products like *Midnight Special* or *Don Kirschner's Rock Concert* or their several imitators couldn't touch Austin City Limits for video and audio quality. It was more than a matter of equipment. Certainly the new U.T. Communications Building could boast state-of-the-art facilities — Robert Schenkkan had done his work well — but so could the L.A. studios. In fact, the show's quality stemmed most importantly from the conscious and determined efforts of producer, director, and camera crew to capture exactly what the musicians wanted to express, without packaging or preconceptions. "It's the only real musician's show on the air," the bands kept saying.

The studio audiences also deserved a measure of credit. Austin concertgoers had in the distant past — previous to the late sixties, say — been charitably described as "lay-down" audiences, meaning that no matter what travesties a performer might commit, he or she could expect a standing ovation. But as music fans became exposed to more and better acts courtesy of the Vulcan Gas Company, the Armadillo, Soap Creek Saloon, Antone's, and the rest of the hot club scene, their musical sophistication improved perceptibly without, however, dampening their energy. So that now it might be more fair, really, to characterize Austin fans as "always

enthusiastic and sometimes knowledgeable," in the words of a kinder critic, than to call them "the most indiscriminate audience this side of the Vatican," as Patrick Carr did once in the *Village Voice*.

The ACL taping sessions now ranked among the best draws in town: Great music and free beer were a winning combination. Audiences therefore tended to be festive and upbeat. In the early years crowds were large, sometimes eight hundred or even a thousand people jamming the bleachers in front of and behind the stage and spilling onto the floor, where they had to contend with the mobile cameras. In a benign frame of mind, and with many of them musically well-informed besides, this audience was a tonic to musicians all too used to playing loud, smoky bars where glasses clinked and rattled and patrons shouted over the music. Nor were ACL's patrons confined to peach-fuzzed and dewy-eyed students. Plenty of weathered country faces showed up in the crowds that poured in during succeeding seasons to hear Mel Tillis or Ernest Tubb or Johnny Paycheck. Sunburned workingmen in hats brought along stout women with strong faces and hands. They came expecting real country music, and they knew it when they heard it.

"A true country audience is by no means a concert audience," wrote Texan Al Reinert in an article on Willie Nelson. "Its daily labor is physical, direct, rarely esthetic, and it takes its pleasures in the same proportions." He meant that the true country audience is usually to be found in the honky-tonks and dance halls. Yet at least part of that time-honored audience seemed to find the atmosphere of Studio 6A perfectly congenial to the music of its jukebox heroes.

Retired Texas Longhorns coach Darrell Royal, of whom it has been said that in Austin "not even the Pope could be more venerated," praises

ACL's audiences as instrumental in the success of the series. He points to George Jones' show as an example of their effect. Frequently and deservedly known as "No-Show Jones," George was scheduled to tape a set in season six, but at the last minute suffered an attack of acute stage fright. Shaky from a recent bout with alcoholism, he simply could not bring himself to leave the shelter of his touring bus. Royal, not for the first time, came to the aid of the show. The legendary football coach, a long-time fan of country music, had befriended a bevy of country musicians, including Jones (not for nothing had Royal once described himself as "Austin's biggest groupie"). Now, exercising his redoubtable skills, he managed to coax Jones out of his bus, into the studio, and finally onto the stage. There he stood, about to bolt, like a deer caught in the headlights. Royal feared the worst. But the audience responded to a hesitant first number with such unfeigned warmth that Jones immediately and visibly relaxed. He went on to give an out-standing performance, then stayed to sign autographs and chat with fans until everyone left for home—for him a rare gesture.

The size of the audience actually represented a victory of sorts by Arhos over Scafe, who had visualized a small, intimate, informal set. Arhos thought informal was fine, but he envisioned something larger, something that would suggest the raucous vitality of a Willie Nelson Fourth of July Picnic, for instance. Well, you couldn't get fifty thousand people into the studio—virtually the minimum required for a Picnic—but you could squeeze in a large enough mass to generate a festive air.

Of course, different artists attracted different kinds of crowds. At the first Doug Sahm show, for example, before smoking was prohibited in the studio, a dense cloud of mostly illegal smoke hung suspended in the cavernous room. The video of that show came out thoroughly purple, as though the acrid tang of marijuana had inspired a sympathetic reaction in the chemicals of the film emulsion. The smoke may also have corroded a few emotional inhibitions, at least in the case of one young woman. Dressed in a full-length gown, she danced dreamily around the studio during most of the session, making her way up front during the last song. Facing the stage as Doug Sahm drove his band to a crescendo, she reached down, grabbed her dress by the hem, and pulled it over her head. She wore nothing beneath it. The scene, for all its drama, had to be left on the cutting room floor.

This loose and relaxed ambience, coupled perhaps paradoxically with a high quality of sound and image, made Austin City Limits an attractive venue. Word leaked out among entertainers: The show was fun to play, and you could project yourself as you wished. Willie Nelson would tell Austin reporter John T. Davis, "I felt like it's hard to get across what we do on a normal TV show. That's why I've done a lot of 'Austin City Limits' shows. They're more geared to concerts. . . . You can present your show in its entirety to the public without interruptions." Besides, he added, "TV is a great way to promote whatever you've got to sell."

Other musicians and their record companies also smelled career enhancement possibilities in the show. A young band named Firefall, for instance, interrupted a national concert tour to fly to Austin and tape ACL, with their label, Atlantic Records, footing the expenses.

Certainly, if musicians came to play it was for love or promotion rather than money. Austin City Limits paid only union scale, about $300 per show to the bandleader (less to the sidemen), and in the early years couldn't even afford to pay hotel expenses. Performers in town to tape ACL usually tried to get bookings at local clubs to help pay their way. Yet it was said that Nelson, for one, refused million-dollar offers from commercial television even while appearing frequently on the PBS series. (Eventually Willie would tape a lengthy "special" for Home Box Office, hiring the ACL producer, director, and crew to shoot it.) The young show was developing a reputation as a musician's dream.

Darrell Royal

Willie Nelson on Nashville session musicians is quoted by Jan Reid, *The Improbable Rise of Redneck Rock* (Austin: Heidelberg Press, 1974; reprint, New York: Da Capo, 1977), p. 306. *Rolling Stone* on the need for a redefinition of country music is quoted by Bane, *Willie*, p. 186. Willis Alan Ramsey's words are from Reid, *Redneck Rock*, p. 175. The Hank Williams quote is from Rufus Jarman, "Country Music Goes to Town," *Nation's Business* 41 (February 1953): 51. Al Reinert's article is "King of Country Music," *New York Times Magazine*, 26 March 1978, pp. 20–28, 50–53. Willie Nelson on the advantages of playing ACL is quoted by Davis, "The Making of Willie's Special."

W
HEN THE THIRD SEASON rolled around, even Chet Atkins called to say he wanted to come and play, clear proof that Austin City Limits was "making it." Atkins, head of RCA's Nashville studios in the fifties, was known as the architect of the Nashville sound that had brought country music out of the rural byways into the mainstream of American popular culture. Nashville had at last become aware that something was happening in Austin, and not only in the clubs.

With the arrival of Chet Atkins, KLRN attracted the attention of the American Federation of Musicians' national office. The union controls certain contractual agreements between its members and music producers, including the PBS network. The Austin station had had its brushes with the AFM's local representatives, but thus

far had managed to elude a point-blank laser-eyed inquiry by the national organization. That was no longer possible with someone like Atkins coming to perform. Here was a highly visible pillar of the Nashville establishment, whose earning power the AFM cherished. If the union let things slide here, it could set a bad precedent. Union executives decreed that the Atkins show would be canceled if KLRN failed to sign the general PBS-AFM contract. And so Austin City Limits entered the union fold. It didn't mean the musicians got paid any better—they were already drawing minimum scale, and that's where they stayed—but it did mean the commencement of a long, ultimately harmonious and productive official relationship between the station and the union.

Thus Austin City Limits continued its uncertain progress. But while the series held its ground nationally, complications arose in Austin, where KLRN-TV suddenly found itself in the midst of political unrest and shifting lines of power. Top brass departed the station, new faces entered, and sharp differences of opinion ensued as to how the show should be handled. Matters grew more confused when a new interpretation of

official state regulations required the station to dissolve its long-standing connection with the University of Texas. No longer, it was declared, could students participate in "internships" at KLRN-TV in exchange for academic credit; the station would become simply a rent-paying tenant of the university. Among other things, this meant the end of a cheap labor supply for ACL.

Luckily for Arhos, serving as both ACL executive producer and KLRN vice-president of programming, he had tenaciousness and a degree of political savvy in his system; he kept his job. Bruce Scafe, by contrast, was not a political animal. He loved jazz and television but had grown a little tired of country music, truth to tell. In fact, he and Arhos had produced and directed a jazz pilot, "Every Tub on Its Own Bottom," with Freddie Hubbard and Pat Metheny, which they hoped would join or replace Austin City Limits as a national series. The PBS system, however, failed to go for it. Weary of political turmoil and experiencing problems in his personal life too, Scafe left before the third season to direct public service programs for the state of Texas.

Staff director Charles Vaughn replaced him. Vaughn was dedicated

**SEASON 3
1978**

301 Michael Murphey
302 Steve Goodman
303 John Prine
304 The Texas Playboys
    Ernest Tubb
305 Chet Atkins
    Merle Travis
306 Doc Watson
    Gove
307 Johnny Rodriguez
    Linda Hargrove
308 John Hartford
    The Dillards
309 Jesse Winchester
    Mother of Pearl
310 Asleep at the Wheel
    Bobby Bridger
311 Vassar Clements
    Gatemouth Brown
312 Merle Haggard
313 Killough & Eckley
    Lost Gonzo Band

to his job but, perhaps mercifully, lacked Scafe's fanatical devotion to perfection. All the same, he too was overworked, serving for much of the year in a dual capacity as producer and director. He therefore began to shift more responsibility to his assistant producer and the show's emcee, Terry Lickona.

Season three witnessed ACL's continuing loyalty to new forms of country music, while it also saw an increase in artists of established national reputation. The first three programs featured the "progressive" sounds of songwriters Michael Murphey, Steve Goodman, and John Prine. Three of the best young songwriters of the day, they helped blur the distinction between country and "folk music." Murphey's "Cosmic Cowboy Souvenir" and "Geronimo's Cadillac" had become anthems for Austin's beer-drinking, long-haired drugstore hippie cowboys, but Murphey himself did not endorse the trend. Indeed, he had moved from Austin to Colorado to get away from the raucous, beer-soaked kids who began to infest the clubs when the Texas legislature dropped the drinking age to eighteen. Austin had changed in five years; these kids just wanted loud boogie music and broken eardrums. A painstaking craftsman who had studied classical Greek metrics, Murphey wrote carefully chiseled lyrics meant to be listened to as poetry. Austin City Limits gave him the forum he wanted. He would appear often on ACL, both solo and with his band. His solo appearance with acoustic instruments in season eight would become a videotape collector's item.

Steve Goodman and John Prine also showed to advantage in the attentive atmosphere of Studio 6A. Numerous artists had covered Goodman's "City of New Orleans"; in Arlo Guthrie's version it hit the pop charts. Yet not many listeners had heard it performed by the Chicago songwriter himself, especially in the

Charles Vaughn

Ernest Tubb

larger context of his work. Goodman's concert was intimate and brilliant. He won the Texas audience completely, and became almost a kind of mascot of the show.

During Goodman's early folksinging days in Chicago, he had met and made friends with John Prine, also making the rounds of the folk circuit. In a spoof of country music clichés, the two once concocted a song that would have "everything" in it: trains, prison, pickup trucks, getting drunk, and mother. The result was "You Never Even Call Me by My Name." David Allan Coe recorded it, adding a stanza of his own, and it made a little headway on the charts, but it was mostly just for fun at concerts. Prine, injecting his music with a country flavor, eventually achieved radio play and success beyond the folk audience. His Austin City Limits concert now gave him room to explore dimensions of humor and subtlety impossible in the three-minute radio song. ACL's potential as a venue for songwriters was beginning to make itself apparent.

(In season ten John Prine would host a poignant program in honor of his friend. Consisting of clips from Steve Goodman's season three appearance plus excerpts from fundraising specials such as "Down Home Country Music," the show constituted ACL's sad tribute to Goodman, who died of cancer in 1984.)

After the three concerts by these emerging songwriters, the third season returned to living C & W history. The Texas Playboys, led by Leon McAuliffe, taped their second ACL show. With three fiddlers — Bob Boatwright, Jack Stidham, and Johnny Gimble — the Playboys soon had grandparents and grandchildren alike clapping in time and dancing in place. The Playboys tape aired with a show by their contemporary Ernest Tubb, a country music pioneer in his own right.

Tubb grew up in Texas, with Jimmie Rodgers his chief inspiration. Along with Floyd Tillman, he helped invent the honky-tonk style that swept country music after World War II. He wrote some of the first "cheatin' songs" in the repertoire, and as a star became a model and father figure for scores of young country singers, including Hank Williams. In the 1970s, though he still played more than 200 road dates a year, he returned nearly every Saturday night to Nashville, where he had been a fixture of the *Grand Ole Opry* and the country music capital for decades. Tubb and his Texas Troubadours, decked out in cowboy hats and boots and yellow scarves, played Studio 6A like the Broken Spoke or any other regular stop on their itinerary. Joking, laughing with the audience, practically kissing babies, Tubb felt as comfortable as an old shoe. His songs—"In the Jailhouse Now" in tribute to Rodgers, his own "Waltz across Texas," and, of course, "Walking the Floor over You"—all brought pure hard-core country music to the advanced videoelectronics of KLRN. The Troubadours were the first band with matching outfits to play Austin City Limits; along with Chet Atkins, Tubb and his band served as advance scouts of establishment credibility.

Chet Atkins, happy to play once the union was satisfied, opened his show with some lovely solos on classical acoustic guitar. Paul Yandell joined him in several duets, including a seventeenth-century composition for Spanish guitar, "Recuerdas de la Alhambra." However, Atkins did not owe his fame to classical picking, and he soon exchanged his acoustic guitar for an electric one. With a piano and rhythm section he'd brought from the Nashville studios, he demonstrated what the Nashville sound was all about. Clean, smooth renditions of pop and country standards, including "Under the Double Eagle," now far removed from its early life as a Texas Czech polka tune, filled the studio. Not content to use every bar chord in the book, Atkins threw in train

whistles and what sounded like every other guitar effect to grace country music since 1950. Atkins enjoyed himself immensely. He later told Johnny Gimble—whose face in the crowd the camera dwelled upon—that "This was the only way to do TV." His show went out with a tape by Merle Travis.

As a boy, Atkins had grown up listening to Merle Travis, whose guitar work stood out so distinctively that "Travis-picking" became a universally recognized style and a major contribution to the Kentucky tradition from which it sprang. Now Travis came to Austin City Limits, sitting on a chair and playing his f-hole hollow-body electric guitar with such brilliance that nobody could remember the dividing line between country and jazz. A prolific and diverse songwriter, Travis had penned some of America's immortal songs, including "Smoke! Smoke! Smoke! (That Cigarette)," a jazz and pop standard of the forties, and Tennessee Ernie Ford's popular hit "Sixteen Tons." Indeed, he had made so much money for Capitol Records that rival RCA hired a young Chet Atkins to compete with him. (The only problem lay in that Atkins was an even less accomplished singer than Travis, who, regardless of his writing talents, would never win any awards as a vocalist.) Travis and Atkins back-to-back on ACL no. 305 amounted to inspired country music history, made all the more valuable by Travis' death a few years later.

As if to continue the history lessons, Travis' occasional cohort and rival guitar virtuoso, Doc Watson, appeared on the following program, accompanied by his son Merle and two other accomplished guitarists, Michael Coleman and Cliff Miller, in an astonishing display of flat-picking. Doc Watson, known for playing fiddle tunes on his guitar, explained that necessity had been the mother of this particular invention. He had once be-

Chet Atkins

Doc Watson

longed to a country-swing band that sometimes played for square dances. Unfortunately, the band lacked a fiddler, so it fell on Doc to play the leads. "Nearly broke my arm," he said. In addition to old-time dance tunes, his ACL set featured pop standards, Nashville tunes, and even a Gershwin song—"Summertime" from *Porgy and Bess*—but they all came out sounding country as mountain dew.

A generation of young folk musicians had learned to play by imitating Doc Watson and Merle Travis. One of them was Gove Scrivenor, whose award-winning show as a one-man band had graced the second season. He returned for an encore; and with shows also by John Hartford and the Dillards, both part of bluegrass music's "new wave," Austin City Limits was starting to look almost like an American folk revival.

But there was more. "Straight country" was represented by Linda Hargrove and Johnny Rodriguez. The bilingual Rodriguez hailed from South Texas and got his break, according to myth, by stealing a goat. The story goes that he got arrested by a Texas Ranger for goat theft. While in jail his singing attracted attention from a kindly sheriff, who arranged for him to work at A. J. "Happy" Shahan's Alamo Village near Bracketville, Texas. There he met Tom T. Hall, who invited him to Nashville. Although time has garbled the details— the goat theft and the meeting with the Texas Ranger are unrelated, for one thing—Rodriguez eventually did wind up in Nashville playing guitar in Hall's band. Now he enjoyed considerable success in his own right. A conspicuous part of his following consisted of women from fourteen to forty, mesmerized by his movie-star looks and mellifluous voice. It didn't harm Rodriguez's popularity either that Willie Nelson, dubbed "the Shakespeare of country music" by Tom T. Hall, rose from the audience and joined him on a couple of songs.

Gatemouth Brown

Gatemouth Brown is a remarkably versatile musician, a man at home on either side of the Texas-Louisiana border. A master of both blues and jazz guitar, he can also make a breakdown fiddle sing. In three appearances on Austin City Limits, he sounded like a different man each time. Brown once said, in an interview with Austin critic Michael Point, "People thought it was sort of strange for a black blues player to be playing country music, but I never could understand that. They must have forgotten that I was raised in Texas around all that music. Bob Wills is as much an influence on my music as anyone, and if people would just listen they'd know that."

Brown will perhaps be longest remembered for his jazz-laced rhythm and blues, a style in which he competed successfully with T-Bone Walker in the 1940s. Jazzmen in his bands have included such luminaries as Jay McShann, Sonny Stitt, and Gene Ammons. On ACL in season two he played Texas country music, but in season three he unleashed a big band, with a sizzling horn section, that forayed into vital and earthy Southwestern jazz. This set went on the air with a thirty-minute segment by Vassar Clements, another man who can play either country or jazz. Bill Arhos had heard Clements playing pure country at the Bottom Line in New York, and on the strength of that brought him to Austin. When Clements hauled out his fiddle at rehearsal and launched into a burst of "hot jazz" à la Stéphane Grappelli and Django Reinhardt, Arhos sat down with his head in his hands. This was not what he had meant at all. Fortunately for him, Clements mixed a few country tunes into that night's set; and in the end artful editing resulted in a primarily country tape.

For many viewers Merle Haggard and the Strangers delivered the season's highlight. The hour-long show clearly demonstrated Haggard's importance to modern country music. Haggard combined it all, from the Lefty Frizzell echoes in the artfully cracked voice to the mournful steel guitar to the Bob Wills-inspired syncopation and hot jazz riffs. (Impressed by Wills, Haggard took up Bob's instrument, the fiddle, and mastered it to the point that he could play it on the album he produced in tribute to Wills.) The Strangers were a big band, with horns (even a trumpet), and they made splendid music that did not confine itself to Nashville hit record formulas. Haggard's flawless performance not only of country ballads but of blues and well-crafted love songs came as a revelation to many of the younger spectators whose acquaintance with his work had gone little further than the jingoistic "Okie from Muskogee." (Commenting on "Okie" during a season seven taping, Haggard would only say, "I was a songwriter and it was an obvious thing to write about.")

Ironically, Haggard's concert almost didn't come to pass. The day of the taping he was stranded in Dallas by sleet and freezing Texas weather. The airlines had canceled scheduled flights, and charters were iffy. Staying in a warm Dallas hotel room looked awfully good. Meanwhile, the Austin City Limits staff, who had spent the day setting up, were getting nervous. Luckily Darrell Royal was on hand. Royal had aided negotiations between ACL and his friend Haggard. The coach got on the phone now and praised the show to the country star. "You'll like it," he promised, assuring Haggard that it was worth a special effort. So the musician found a limousine and an off-duty fireman to drive him to Austin, where he discovered that Royal was right. Since then Haggard has returned frequently, both with his band and solo.

(After that first show, Haggard repaired to Royal's house, where Charlie Duke, the astronaut, was also

Willie Nelson

Merle Haggard

visiting. Duke lived in nearby New Braunfels. When Duke had been slated to fly to the moon, Haggard, hearing that he liked country music, went into the studio and cut a personal tape for him to take along—it contained, naturally, "Silver Wings." Duke played the tape on the flight, once going and once coming, but had never met Haggard personally. Now, at Royal's house, he punched the tape machine, remarking that it was his first time to play the tape on earth. What should come up but "Silver Wings." It was a memorable moment.)

The season finished closer to home, with a program featuring the folk-rock of Killough and Eckley, and the high-energy Austin sounds of Gary P. Nunn, Bob Livingston, and the rest of the Lost Gonzo Band, now divorced from Jerry Jeff Walker and out on their own. The Gonzos' tape captured much of the infectious high spirits that made their live performances so delightful, but seldom seemed to translate well to their records.

The third season thus continued the eclectic booking policy Joe Gracey had set in the first year. The series, however, was reaching out perceptibly from its regional base in Austin and the Southwest, going as far as Nashville and beyond to bring in performers from the national circuit. The musicians Austin City Limits brought in almost without exception exemplified, either historically or as revivalists, the authentic current of traditional American music. Altogether there were twenty-two acts on thirteen programs that year—an impressive achievement for a series whose entire budget was less than that of a single episode of *Charlie's Angels*.

Gatemouth Brown was interviewed by Michael Point, "Borrowed Guitar Starts Bluesman to Stardom," *Austin American-Statesman,* 13 August 1985, *Onward* magazine, p. 26.

THE FOURTH SEASON of Austin City Limits stands out in some respects as its most curious; it was at any rate an important watershed. Notably, it marked Terry Lickona's debut as producer. Lickona was born in Dutchess County, New York, in 1947, twenty years before Timothy Leary achieved notoriety in the same county. At college Lickona worked as a deejay, then moved to an FM rock station in Poughkeepsie, his hometown. When the station abruptly changed to a country format, he tried to ease the transition by playing rock with a country flavor, and vice versa. Acts like the Flying Burrito Brothers, the Grateful Dead, and Waylon Jennings got a lot of air time. If Lickona had been spinning platters for KOKE-FM in Austin, he would have called what he played progressive country music.

Lickona knew about Austin. He had a friend attending school there who kept him informed about the city's heady musical delights. The friend suggested he come down for Willie Nelson's Fourth of July Picnic. So in the summer of 1974 Lickona found himself in Bryan, Texas, home of Texas A&M University and the Texas Speedway, where 100,000 people had congregated to broil themselves while listening to an impressive line-up of country stars, rock stars, regional stars, and Willie's friends. For three days the music played. The banked oval racetrack cut off the faintest breeze, but let in the Texas July sun just fine. "Shit-kicker outdoor agonies," novelist Bill Brammer called these tests of endurance which somehow had become the Texas answer to Monterey, Woodstock, and the other pop festivals of a bygone era. Although the audience at the First Annual Dripping Springs Reunion of 1972 had included a sizable percentage of working folk who came to hear Roy Acuff, Loretta Lynn, Ernest Tubb, and other country music legends, the proportions had changed. The audience now consisted mostly of youngsters who came to see Leon Russell and similar idols of the rock pantheon and who likely had never heard of Bob Wills, let alone Milton Brown. Still, once

through the gates they became a captive audience and so were exposed, willy-nilly, to a musical education by modern country artists like Billy Joe Shaver or Tompall Glaser.

Lickona liked Texas so much he decided to stay. He managed finally to land a job in Austin with KUT-FM, the public radio station housed under the same roof as KLRN-TV. Still interested in country-rock music, and perceiving that the future lay in television, he became a regular at ACL taping sessions. In 1977, the third year of series production, Lickona walked in and volunteered his services. Since ACL was still operating on a shoestring, with no single person committed to it full-time, management made him assistant producer, announcer, and general "gofer" under Charles Vaughn. Vaughn was doubling as both producer and director, while Bill Arhos and Howard Chalmers split executive producer's chores. As the season wore on, however, it became apparent that the double load of producer and director was too much for Vaughn, or anyone, to handle, and more responsibility shifted to Lickona, who took on booking duties and expanded his role into other areas as well.

SEASON 4
1979

401 Norton Buffalo

402 John McEuen & Friends

403 Dan Del Santo
     Taj Mahal

404 Neville Brothers Band
     Robert Shaw
     Lightnin' Hopkins

405 Nashville Super Pickers
     Tom T. Hall

406 Leon Redbone
     Steve Fromholz

407 Tom Waits

408 Delbert McClinton
     Cate Brothers

409 Pure Prairie League
     Bobby Bare

410 Alvin Crow
     Marcia Ball

411 Hoyt Axton

412 Little Joe y La Familia
     Esteban Jordan

413 Doug Kershaw
     Clifton Chenier

In 1978 and 1979 the station went through a number of changes. For one thing, it separated from its sister station in San Antonio, changing its call letters and channel number in the process. Beginning in May 1979 the Austin station would become KLRU, Channel 18. Second, people began playing musical chairs at the management level. Robert Schenkkan retired, Howard Chalmers left the station, Charles Vaughn left the show, and Bill Arhos entered a state of temporary severance from ACL production. Terry Lickona was quick to see a void. Fearing that someone from "outside" might be imported to produce Austin City Limits, now growing into quite a popular program, he entered the new station manager's office, talked very fast, and emerged with a deal. If he would produce the station's annual fund-raising auction — a wearisome and thankless task — the station would give him a shot at producing Austin City Limits. He did, and it did. Lickona signed on to produce season four. Clark Santee, from WITF-TV in Harrisburg, Pennsylvania, would direct.

Lickona underwent a form of baptism by fire. Continuing to handle booking, he brought in an array of artists that even by ACL standards was unusual. Not all of them reflected the new producer's choice. He was becoming educated in the vicissitudes of the music business. He wanted Leon Redbone, for example, but since Redbone's manager was also Tom Waits' manager, he got Waits as well. They taped their shows the same night. Waits had a considerably more pop-oriented style than ACL viewers might have expected, but he delivered a solid and coherent performance. Redbone, on the other hand, an elusive and brilliant performer of old-time music, used film clips and other visuals to re-create the feel of the ragtime music era. MTV should be so good. (Redbone also, inexplicably, said he would not play if there were people behind his peripheral vision. Since many seats did indeed encroach upon the stage perimeters, his demand caused consternation. The staff nevertheless accommodated him, turning away scores of ticket-holders who, understandably, expressed something substantially less than happiness.)

The station's new management decided the show needed a new look, something more in keeping with the idea of a national show. Director Santee accordingly introduced color gels and star filters. Star filters turn spotlights into bright, four-pronged stars smiling down from the firmament. They are very popular at rock concerts because they contribute heavily to an atmosphere of flash and glitter. They achieved the same effect in Studio 6A; with the place awash in blues and reds, it was possible to suppose that one had been beamed abruptly into Las Vegas. *Showtime!* The effect was not necessarily bad for pop performers like Tom Waits or Taj Mahal or even the Neville Brothers, but it was more than a little disconcerting when slashed over the plain honest blues of Robert Shaw or the Panhandle swing of Alvin Crow. And, of course, it would have given Paul Bosner apoplexy.

The look of the set changed too. Santee added a few pieces to the set design and put the audience out front, in a more conventional relationship to the performers. No longer did the audience share the stage, lapping the musicians in intimacy. Whereas the lights had previously illuminated performers and audience more or less impartially, now they highlighted the performer and left the audience in shadow, underscoring the psychological distance between them. Finally, the cameras now focused almost exclusively on the musicians, going in often for close-ups, and only sporadically cutting away to a pretty girl or the audience clapping between songs. Bosner's concept of performer and audience as equal participants in a performance event was vanishing.

Moreover, a serious problem arose with the beer: There was none. The university's president, Lorene Rogers, thought it unseemly for alcoholic beverages to be served on the university campus. And free yet! Lone Star Beer gallantly continued to underwrite the show, but the beerless studio audiences grew markedly stiffer than in years previous, despite the colored lights. The following season, after much heroic bureaucratic infighting, the beer returned, but then only on condition that the station seek special permission to roll out the barrels for each concert.

The viewing season led off, to the surprise of many followers, with a one-hour set by Norton Buffalo. Though a harmonica wizard and interesting blues musician, the young Buffalo could scarcely claim to be a household word. Neither did he belong to the camp of obscure Austin "progressive country" musicians. Originally, Levon Helm and the RKO All-Stars had been slated to fill half the program. Therein lies a story. Helm, former stalwart of The Band, a musical cornerstone of the sixties, came to town late in the taping season for his concert. It was December; the series would go on the air in January. The RKO All-Stars trekked faithfully to the studio for a sound check in the afternoon. Levon did not accompany them, but that was not unusual; singers often chose to skip rehearsals. By showtime, however, he still had not arrived. With a packed studio, and the band waiting anxiously in the dressing room, Helm's manager confided to Lickona that they had a problem. Life appeared to be imitating art — in this case, The Band's early hit "Stage Fright." Levon Helm had stage fright, a bad case of it. The thought of facing TV cameras paralyzed him; he swore he couldn't leave his hotel room. Lickona's persuasiveness availed nothing. And so

Austin City Limits had to reluctantly cancel a show featuring the future co-star of the movie *Coal Miner's Daughter.* It was Lickona's task, of course, to break the news to the expectant studio audience.

The gamut of talent ran from pure folk to pure pop, with several brands of country music in between. In the folk arena, John McEuen, the driving force behind the (Nitty Gritty) Dirt Band, hosted what amounted to an old-time hootenanny with string band virtuosos Vassar Clements, Byron Berline, and Bryan Savage, to mention only a few of the all-star cast. Reels, jigs, and hoedowns, laced with a lyrical flute accompaniment, filled the air. Musicians and audience both appeared to exceed the legal limits on fun, despite the beer ban. As a special surprise McEuen introduced Elizabeth Cotten, author of "Freight Train" and a living link to the black folk tradition. Unaccompanied except by her own guitar and looking like the grandmother of every child's dreams, Cotten held the largely student audience spellbound. Even under the gaudy lights the evening came alive with a gentle magic. The tape drew critical raves and remains a standout not only of that season but of the entire series.

A casual viewer might have wondered about ACL's direction when tuning in the following week to encounter the steel drums and Caribbean rhythms of Taj Mahal, then in his calypso period, pulsating under the star filters. A concert by Dan Del Santo and the Professors of Pleasure (including for the evening Tomás Ramírez and Johnny Gimble) accompanied Taj's tape. Del Santo's music displayed startling diversity in its own right, proceeding from an eloquent dobro solo to jazz to reggae to juju. (Some years later Del Santo would host a KUT-FM radio show called *World Beat,* on which he would endeavor to educate Austinites to the subtleties of Afro-Caribbean music.)

One highly unusual hour, with its own strange unity, featured the Neville Brothers Band *and* Robert Shaw *and* Lightnin' Hopkins. Natives of New Orleans and highly conscious of their roots, the Neville Brothers incorporated a 30-year family heritage of Dixieland, blues, and early rock, fused into a unique and very danceable blend. No one offers a better introduction to the special New Orleans sound than the Neville Brothers. Asked what makes New Orleans music so unique, Aaron Neville told Michael Point, "It's not just playing the notes, it's playing all the music behind the notes. . . . You've got to know what the music means to really play it well."

Lickona also tried hard to get New Orleans greats Fats Domino and Professor Longhair for Austin City Limits. Professor Longhair was a pianist who possessed one of the purest and most important New Orleans boogie-woogie styles, a link between early ragtime jazz piano and rock and roll. Longhair suffered neglect by the record industry, but every notable musician in the Crescent City paid court to the Professor. His rhythms could make a dead man dance. One of his best albums, *Live on the Queen Mary,* came about because Paul McCartney flew him to California to play a party on the old dry-docked ship, and had the good sense to switch on a tape recorder.

Fats Domino, of course, won commercial success by translating the primitive strains of pure New Orleans rhythm and blues into a rock beat that galvanized the white teenagers of the nation. Unfortunately for ACL, neither Domino nor Longhair much wanted to leave the comforts of that pleasant city, and Lickona's deals fell through, even though tickets had already been printed up for Fats. Fats, the Professor, and the Nevilles could hardly have been surpassed as a window on the infectious New Orleans mix, itself the genesis of so much modern American music. Professor Longhair died not long thereafter, in 1980. Because practically no film footage of Longhair exists — even his recorded output was small, thanks to shameful treatment by record companies — the ACL near-miss was especially grievous.

Robert Shaw and Lightnin' Hopkins represented Texas' own living blues history. Probably the last of the great barrelhouse piano players, Shaw had learned his trade in the steamy East Texas brothels and road-houses of the Prohibition era. He married and settled in Austin and became a respectable businessman, but remained in constant demand for his driving, rollicking blues style and repertoire of old ragtime tunes. Shaw claimed to be the only man left who knew some of those barrelhouse songs, and no one could dispute him. Always friendly, unpretentious, and direct, Shaw performed brilliantly on Austin City Limits, despite the slightly incongruous Steinway baby grand and the blazing spotlights.

Sam "Lightnin'" Hopkins could not always be said to be unpretentious and direct, but his central importance to Texas urban blues earned him a lot of leeway. Born in the country, Lightnin' began playing professionally after World War II, in Houston, where he honed a haunting guitar style, a gravelly voice, and a gift for lyrics that cut straight to the bone. He also acquired a penchant for sartorial splendor. On ACL, sporting a dapper hat, tinted glasses, powder-blue Western togs, three enormous diamond rings on his right hand, and a gold tooth, the musician proved a match for the stagelights. His music sparkled, too.

As with so many American blues artists, talent and fame failed to bring financial success to Lightnin'. Chiseling club owners and booking agents had taught him hard lessons. He had learned not to accept checks, and he did not give credit. Unaware of Lightnin's policy, the ACL staff had neglected to have cash on hand to pay him. Now it was Sunday night with the banks long closed. The show's star continued to insist on cold American dollars up front, and his manager intimated there wouldn't be much of a concert without them. The station had no money. The staff conferred, and at length dug deep into their own pockets to produce the green. And Lightnin' played.

Lightnin' Hopkins died in 1982, Robert Shaw in 1985. With their deaths, and those of other ACL performers such as Merle Travis, Ernest Tubb, and Marty Robbins, the value of the Austin City Limits tapes as archival documents becomes clear. Performances can last as long as the mylar on which they are captured. Unedited footage and "outtakes" are preserved also, a practice sure to be regarded by future folklorists and musicologists as a distinct boon. Naturally, all the great musicians whom the show has "missed" come to mind, not only Professor Longhair but the Armadillo's own Freddy King, the great Texas songster Mance Lipscomb, the aging pioneer Cajun fiddlers — everyone will have a different list.

But ACL's producers have never been interested in mere antiquarianism. During the show's fourth year Nashville came to town in the persons of Tom T. Hall, Bobby Bare, and the "Nashville Super Pickers." A more perfect selection of Nashville's session men than the "Super Pickers" would be hard to find. The group included Johnny Gimble on fiddle and mandolin, Buddy Emmons on pedal steel, Hargus "Pig" Robbins on piano, Phil Baugh on standard guitar, Charlie McCoy on harmonica, Russell Hicks on rhythm guitar and second steel, Henry Strzelecki on bass, and Buddy Harman on drums. These men had supplied the Nashville sound for virtually every C & W artist who recorded during the fifties and sixties.

For until Willie Nelson and his sidekicks began making waves, it was unheard of for stars to use their road bands in the studio. And it wasn't hard to see why the Nashville sound had dominated the industry: These guys played "clean as country water," as John Sebastian once observed. It would not be easy for a conservative record executive to take a chance on an unfamiliar band, knowing that the technical perfection of session men like these could be had for the asking and the fee.

As geologists use road cuts to study a site's sedimentary history, so might the country music student use the Nashville Pickers tape. It amounts to a virtual core sample of nearly everything hillbilly, from Southeastern mountain music to Southwestern dance hall music, from hoedown to honky-tonk, from "Rollin' in My Sweet Baby's Arms" to "Faded Love." The show opened with Gimble's rendition of the Bob Wills classic, then in round robin form showcased the talents of each musician, from the country/jazz steel guitar stylings of Buddy Emmons to the country/blues harp of Charlie McCoy, all played with classic virtuosity. The concert enjoyed a second incarnation as a record on the Flying Fish label, titled, of course, *Live from Austin City Limits*.

Tom T. Hall and Bobby Bare are both master storytellers and, these days, ranking members of the Nashville music industry. The latter condition was not always the case. Both put in time at Tootsie's Orchid Lounge in Nashville in the early sixties, hanging out with other songwriters who had more talent than money such as Hank Cochran, Mel Tillis, Harlan Howard, and Willie Nelson. Eventually such well-crafted songs as "Old Dogs, Children, and Watermelon Wine," "Ballad of Forty Dollars," and "The Year That Clayton Delaney Died" brought commercial success and a reputation as the intellectual's country musician to Hall (he has published a novel, too, *The Laughing Man of Woodmont Cave*). Of course, he also penned the nauseously sentimental "I Love (Little Baby Ducks . . . etc.)," but mercifully left it out of his ACL show. Debonair in pinstriped suit, vest, and tie, with his band, the Storytellers, decked out in matching sequined outfits, Hall mixed his best songs with anecdotes about how they came to be written. Bobby Bare, with hits like "Detroit City," "Miller's Cave," and "Marie Laveau," has also gained great popularity and commensurate material reward without losing his down-home country ways. A favorite of Austin audiences, he returned to ACL in season six, and has appeared on several specials.

Steve Fromholz, Marcia Ball, Alvin Crow, and Delbert McClinton looked like ACL regulars as each taped another show. But fresh faces appeared, too. Some belonged to Hoyt Axton, the Cate Brothers, and Pure Prairie League. The music of the Cate Brothers and Pure Prairie marked an experimental return to purism in Southern country music. Some journalists tagged it "progressive country," in fact, but it bore only a distant kinship to the Austin variety.

Actually, by 1979 Austin's touted progressive country movement had virtually run its course, with musical energy flowing into rock, jazz, and older country-western forms. Kinky Friedman and the Texas Jewboys had moved to New York to become the house band at Manhattan's trendy Lone Star Café. Greezy Wheels had dissolved, the Gonzos had broken up, and other "redneck rock" musicians had branched off in new directions. Alvin Crow referred to his music as "regressive country," a nearly pure mixture of honky-tonk and Western Swing that attracted not only young people, but also the older generation of Saturday night dancers and clubgoers who had been left to languish when country turned to rock. Oldtimers and old music were enjoying a new lease on life. Austin music, still intensely vital, was entering another state of flux and ferment.

The fourth ACL season closed out a long way from Norton Buffalo or Tom Waits. The last two programs featured *conjunto* greats Little Joe y la Familia and Esteban Jordan, the latter of whom music critic Joe Nick Patoski once dubbed "the Jimi Hendrix of *conjunto*"; and high-energy Louisiana music by Clifton Chenier and the "Rockin' Cajun," Doug Kershaw. There could be little question of calling these musicians "progressive country" or "mainstream country" or trying to fit them into any well-known commercial category. They represented pure musical energy, resistant to labels, expressing itself in ways that spoke directly to their respective Chicano and Cajun cultures. Folklorists appreciate such forms as belonging to the "vernacular idiom," in contrast to the dominant society's relatively standardized cultural expressions. The term relates, of course, to the historical distinction between the modern vernacular languages (and their literatures), and the old "high" literary languages such as Latin. In a way, one could almost describe the entirety of country music as "vernacular," at least when compared to the mainstream of American popular music, though that might be stretching the term a bit. Anyway, Terry Lickona was no folklorist. He did, however, feel that a strong element of "roots music" was critical to the ACL magic.

Lickona thus found his maiden season as producer occasionally rocky going. The talent varied widely, ranging from unknown Austin groups to some of Nashville's most famous pickers, from primitive gutbucket hollers to sophisticated jazz, from pure blues to slick pop. Whether a central concept lurked behind the hodgepodge was hard to tell; serendipity and grabbag seemed the operating principles of selection as much as anything else did. Still, out of this improbable mélange would eventually emerge a formula that would keep Austin City Limits alive longer than any other music television show to date.

Aaron Neville was interviewed by Michael Point, "Nevilles Fuse Music of Bayou," *Austin American-Statesman,* 20 June 1985.

THE PACE TOOK ITS TOLL on the new director, Clark Santee. Like Vaughn before him, Santee was first a television man, not a music devotee. He did not possess inexhaustible tolerance for the numberless petty details that go into successfully capturing on tape a high-quality concert performance. Changes in the editing process that year did nothing to ease Santee's load, either.

When the station's editing machines broke down, Santee and Hough took the videotapes and rough sound mix and flew to Opryland Studios in Nashville. Opryland, a television spin-off of WSM radio, mother of the *Grand Ole Opry,* boasted something called the CMX editing system, new and computerized state-of-the-art technology. All the Nashville TV music programs took their film to Opryland for editing. Santee, Hough, and the studio technicians blitzed through all thirteen ACL shows — twenty-three videotapes — in less than a week. The rush job did not encourage the high quality of post-production work that had distinguished the previous three years. In a hurry, Santee permitted some questionable editing decisions. With the season over, tired, and with personal matters demanding attention, he decided to resign. David Hough, who had been aboard almost since the show emerged from the gleam in Bosner's eye, was growing weary himself, and considered following Santee's example.

At this point there occurred another key event in ACL's evolution: Allan Muir joined the troupe as director. Based in Los Angeles, the bearded, free-wheeling Muir was known as a musician's director. He had worked with Arthur Fiedler, Jim Croce, Sonny Rollins, Freddy King, Judy Collins, Cat Stevens, and Henry Mancini among others. He had directed episodes of *Don Kirschner's Rock Concert* and *Midnight Special;* he had two Emmys under his belt. One of them he had won in 1971 for a rock special, "Leon Russell and Friends"; the second he had earned in 1973 for "The Plot to Overthrow Christmas," produced at PBS station KCET-TV in Los Angeles. No stranger to Austin or KLRU, Muir had directed some episodes of *Carrascolendas* about the time Austin City Limits was starting up. Bruce Scafe knew and admired Muir's work; he had patterned some of his own ideas on *The Session* after Muir's. Muir shared with Scafe a great fondness for music; in high school and college he had played drums and trombone.

Muir contributed a ballast that the show needed. Hough, excited, dropped his thoughts about leaving. As for Lickona, his first season's battles had helped crystallize his sense of what the series needed to nail down a secure berth in the ratings. The realization had dawned that he was, indeed, the producer of Austin City Limits; the buck largely stopped with him. True, the executive producer held veto power, but it was really the producer's sense of style that would finally stamp the program. The producer was responsible for bringing all the elements together — the talent, the set, the equipment, the camera crew and technicians. Though he could not do everything himself, he pretty much had the last word. Lickona therefore decided, since the praise or blame would be his anyway, to exercise greater control, from pre-production through final editing.

Allan Muir, Terry Lickona

Though season four had perhaps erred on the side of eclectic excess, Lickona thought he saw in it the seeds of a successful formula, one that would balance out the show's trademarks. The line-up would be diverse, but country-oriented; it would include both national acts and local bands, and it would try to relate to Southwestern musical roots. Such a recipe, he fervently hoped, would produce a winner. Bill Arhos, who was still peddling the show in the yearly PBS sweepstakes even though he was not involved in production, hoped so too.

One major theme of the series, its attention to songwriters, would be consolidated in a landmark show of the fifth season. To some extent this emphasis had existed from the beginning, when ACL was drawing heavily on the Austin talent pool, for the solo singer/songwriters had formed the mainstay of progressive country. Steve Goodman's and John Prine's successful solo acts in season three, not to mention Jesse Winchester's beautiful work, had further proved Studio 6A's attractiveness for serious writers. And now a blockbuster "Songwriters Special," featuring six of C&W's best-known writers, occupied center stage. It was a country music aficionado's dream come true. Willie Nelson, Floyd Tillman, Hank Cochran, Sonny Throckmorton, Red Lane, and Whitey Shafer sat in a semicircle with acoustic guitars, picking and singing as casually as if they were in somebody's living room. And indeed, the show was more or less a picking session that spilled over from Darrell Royal's house, where musicians flying in to play had congregated for the preceding two days. Even Ray Price, who happened to be in the studio audience, joined in the act. They all had such a good time they decided to come back and do it again the next year.

Ray Charles' show went down as a major event also. By a combination of hard work and good luck Lickona managed to book his long-time idol, Charles, accompanied by his orchestra and the Raelettes. Charles starred in the only one-hour show of the fifth season devoted to a single artist. The concert glittered, with ample room for the singer to showcase his contributions to rhythm and blues, soul, and country (his 1962 album, *Modern Sounds in Country and Western Music*, and his No. 1 single, "I Can't Stop Loving You," were among country music's first crossover hits). The colored lights and nightclub atmosphere — Muir had modified the star filter approach but had not abandoned it — suited the Ray Charles Show perfectly; nightclubs, after all, were his natural habitat. Charles' concert boosted staff morale; it was a feather in ACL's collective cap. Equally important, the singer's great crossover appeal brought the series to the attention of a larger, more pop-oriented section of the national audience.

An interesting backstage adventure marked Ray Charles' visit. In addition to musicians and football players, millions of bats make Austin their home, and a colony of them found the cavernous limestone Communications Building a comfortable residence. Ordinarily they caused no trouble, but on the night of Charles' show one of them strayed into his dressing room. The singer's manager insisted that the room wasn't big enough for both Ray and the bat; one or the other had to go. Fortunately, a flurry of broom-waving convinced the bat to leave, freeing Charles to perform.

Contrasting dramatically with the worldly nightclub strains of Ray Charles and the Raelettes was the high lonesome sound of Ralph Stanley and the Clinch Mountain Boys. Stanley, the "Doctor of Bluegrass Music," was a country music patriarch. He and his brother Carter, powerfully influenced by Bill Monroe and his legendary Blue Grass Boys — Car-

Ray Charles

**SEASON 5
1980**

501   Roy Clark &
      Gatemouth Brown

502   Don Williams
      Janie Fricke

503   Songwriters Special:
      Willie Nelson
      Floyd Tillman
      Hank Cochran
      Sonny Throckmorton
      Red Lane
      Whitey Shafer

504   Ray Charles

505   Ralph Stanley
      Uncle Walt's Band

506   Joe Ely
      Jerry Jeff Walker

507   Hank Williams, Jr.
      Shake Russell Band

508   Johnny Gimble
      Texas Swing Pioneers

509   Johnny Paycheck
      Billy Joe Shaver

510   Flaco Jimenez
      Beto & Los Fairlanes

511   Moe Bandy &
      Joe Stampley
      Marty Robbins

512   Carl Perkins
      Joe Sun

513   Mel Tillis
      Gail Davies

ter had played in Monroe's band — had created an even more tradition-based music than Monroe. Their 1950s recordings had fascinated an entire younger generation of folk revivalists. Carter died in 1966, but Ralph carried on with a succession of musicians. (One of them, Ricky Skaggs, would himself play ACL in the seventh and tenth seasons.) Now the banjo-picking Ralph and the new Clinch Mountain Boys proceeded to galvanize the studio with bluegrass and string-band mountain tunes like "Little Maggie" and a cappella country gospel numbers sung in close harmony. The music thrilled its audience, even though some found it jarring to hear "Weep Not, Friends, I'm Going Home," a song that seemed to cry out for a little church in the woodlands, amid a sea of colored spotlights more appropriate to Ray Charles.

Bill Monroe, the undisputed father of bluegrass, would himself appear on ACL several times over the years. His Blue Grass Boys had at one time or another included Earl Scruggs and Lester Flatt, Sonny Osborne, Chubby Wise, Cedric Rainwater, Carter Stanley, Jimmy Martin, Don Reno, Vassar Clements, Peter Rowan, and many others — a veritable who's who of bluegrass. In ACL's eleventh season, after more than a half-century of playing professionally, Monroe led an all-star cast of bluegrass greats in a grand summation of the genre. These included brothers Jim and Jesse (Mc-Reynolds), Mac Wiseman, and Ralph Stanley, any one of whom could have fronted a memorable show of his own. Bluegrass admirers will give thanks for this tape for a long time to come.

Monroe is a contemporary of the musicians who created western swing in the 1930s. If his and Stanley's work took listeners back to Southeastern country music's roots, then the Texas Swing Pioneers program offered an equivalent education in Southwest-

ern musical history. Johnny Gimble ramrodded the affair. The ubiquitous Gimble, one of Bob Wills' Texas Playboys in the mid-forties, possesses an abiding interest in old-time music. After talking to Lickona, who needed little convincing, he rounded up surviving veterans of Milton Brown and His Musical Brownies, the Light Crust Doughboys, Cliff Bruner's Texas Wanderers, the Bar-X Cowboys, and the Rose City Swingsters to play a special show as the Texas Swing Pioneers. The Pioneers included Frank Reneau, Cliff Bruner, Zeke Campbell, Deacon Anderson, Smokey Montgomery, Eldon Shamblin, Jerry and Johnny Gimble, Bill Mounce, Curly Hollinsworth, and J. R. Chatwell, a who's who of Texas swingers. Since Western Swing, in contrast to Southeastern music, was above all dance-hall music, the crew set up a dance floor in front of the stage. (In the Deep South, where the Bible exerted a stronger influence than in Texas, people frowned on dancing, which helps explain why the farther west of the Mississippi you travel, the more dance halls you'll find.)

Although now in their sixth, seventh, and even eighth decades, the swing musicians immediately broke into a hot dance beat that soon had the young people on the floor sweating and grinning. As with the original Texas Playboys show, it was the first time most of them had played together since before World War II. But their timing and phrasing sounded as though there had never been a break. No toothless relic from some musty Smithsonian, this music bristled with raunch and bite. The evening ended all too quickly for both band and audience. On a tide of good spirits, the Pioneers followed up by entering the Dallas studio where the Playboys had cut *For the Last Time*. There, joined by "Papa" Calhoun, who had skipped the trip to Austin, they recorded a double album. The cover features an excellent photo of the ACL stage set for season five.

Austin City Limits, midway through its first decade, had tasted success and found it sweet. Some of the most famous entertainers in the music business were clamoring to be on the show, despite miniscule wages. They knew it was good exposure, and great fun besides. Lickona had to fight to hold a berth for the local and the unorthodox acts that, he believed, constituted an essential ingredient in the programming brew: something old, something new, something regional and something national; something from the mainline and the sidetrack too. He wanted viewers to feel they could tune in to Austin City Limits and always catch an interesting show, something unlikely to appear anywhere else.

Some performers, though willing to play Austin City Limits, are screened from Lickona and his agents by solicitous managers who feel less than ecstatic about the pay. Lickona had long wanted Loretta Lynn, for example, but couldn't contact her. His calls were not returned. Eventually he encountered her traveling companion, to whom he explained his dilemma. No problem, she said. She was driving Loretta to the dentist that afternoon, and would relay the message. And that's how Loretta Lynn brought her elaborate stage show to ACL in season eight. When she and her manager saw the playback, they agreed it was her best television appearance. Lynn didn't cash the $400 check she received for her work; she returned it to PBS as a donation, and said she wanted to play the show again.

Loretta's gesture, however, is not altogether typical of performers. Leon Russell's attitude provides a good contrast. "Why should I give away my show for free?" he querulously answered an invitation. "It's too far to travel for no money."

Over the second five years some extraordinary talent indeed would grace the KLRU studio, from George Jones to Leo Kottke, from Charley

Tammy Wynette

Loretta Lynn

Pride to Joe "King" Carrasco, from Tammy Wynette to Bonnie Raitt. Pure blues poured from B. B. King, and jazz from Pete Fountain. By chance or design, a virtual rockabilly retrospective took place, with Carl Perkins, Roy Orbison, Ray Campi, and Sleepy LaBeef, not to mention "The Killer" himself, Jerry Lee Lewis, all showing up at one time or another to dazzle youngsters hardly born when the stars had their heyday.

The Texas Swing Pioneers' great triumph inspired several successors. In season six the David Grisman Quintet, a young bluegrass/jazz group, hosted an old-timers' "Mandolin Special" with Tiny Moore, Jethro Burns, and — again — Johnny Gimble, who traded his fiddle for a mandolin. Virtuosos Moore and Burns had been pillars of country music since the forties. Moore had played with many bands, including the Texas Playboys, while Burns had gained fame for his role in the great comedy team Homer and Jethro. His ACL performance enlightened those who might have thought he could only crack jokes; the Mandolin Special produced some of the best string band jazz of the series.

Another lively and historically important show occurred in the ninth season (1984). Called "Country Legends," it featured long-time *Grand Ole Opry* stars Kitty Wells, Pee Wee King, Faron Young, Joe and Rose Maphis, and the Sons of the Pioneers. The gathering seemed like a family reunion. Pee Wee King, author of "Tennessee Waltz," the song many writers credit with transforming country into popular music, played accordion and performed his masterpiece accompanied by "Redd" Stewart on guitar and the Collins Sisters singing backup vocals. "Queen of Country Music" Kitty Wells sang a stirring "Dust on the Bible (Will Doom Your Poor Soul)" and, of course, her immortal "It Wasn't God Who Made Honky-Tonk Angels." Guitar wizard Joe Maphis, author of the beer-drinker's anthem "Dim Lights, Thick Smoke, and Loud, Loud Music," played his double-neck guitar and accompanied his wife Rose Lee. They performed "Nine-Pound Hammer" in memory of Merle Travis. The pedal steel guitar of Jimmy Day, a 1950s honky-tonk song trademark, along with Johnny Gimble's fiddle, without which no old-timers' jubilee would be complete, lent further character to the revival.

But the legendary Sons of the Pioneers stopped the show. The Pioneers, whose most famous alumnus is probably Roy Rogers, began singing their cowboy songs in the early 1930s. They have never disbanded, although many musicians have passed through the group. Their vocal harmonies won them early fame, and the Pioneers' instrumental breaks have consistently featured some of country music's most exciting jazz melodies. Their ACL appearance recalled the adventurousness of 1930s "country jazz." Alongside such Pioneers classics as "Cool Water" and "Tumbling Tumbleweeds," songs by such gospel-pop groups as the Oak Ridge Boys (on ACL in season ten) sounded flat and one-dimensional. At least one influential rock group of the seventies, the New Riders of the Purple Sage, could trace their lineage directly to the Sons of the Pioneers by way of their namesake, the ("Old") Riders of the Purple Sage, who accompanied Roy Rogers during much of his movie career. In the 1980s, Riders in the Sky (on ACL in season six) were another group who made a living by adopting the Pioneers' style and updating the cowboy theme.

Faron Young, "The Singing Sheriff," contributed to the program with songs and tales of Tootsie's Orchid Lounge, notably the oft-told story about his buying "Hello, Walls" from a young unknown writer named Willie Nelson. Finally, the entire cast came out to close the show with the old gospel rave-up "I Saw the Light." It was a

great way to get your country music history.

The Austin City Limits context has proved a songwriters' delight: quiet, attentive audiences, no distractions, excellent acoustics, a relaxed atmosphere. For their part, singer/songwriters offer a sympathetic subject to the production crew: A solo artist performing with feeling affords a perceptive camera operator and an intuitive director the opportunity for skilled and creative close-ups. Here public television can live up to its promise of delivering honest art free of commercial distortions. It's no wonder that, as ACL associate producer Susan Caldwell remarks, "All the great songwriters want to do our show."

Whether purposefully or not, the emphasis on songwriters tied in closely with an interest in country music basics. Songwriters such as Ernest Tubb, Floyd Tillman, and Merle Travis had fueled the music's commercial expansion in the 1940s, and Hank Williams, another powerful songwriter, had nudged it into more popular acceptance in the early 1950s.

The rock explosion of the middle fifties, however, plunged the industry into the doldrums, a situation that Chet Atkins and his session men sought to combat by developing the "Nashville sound" (though Atkins later admitted to some misgivings). They wanted to cleanse the music of its "hillbilly" associations and make it more palatable to the middle-class listener. They tried to smooth over the old country roughness, adding strings and saccharine backup vocals to "sweeten" the already slick formulas of Music Row's studio musicians. They succeeded; the new sound did indeed appeal to a new type of listener. Not a country audience — those people still liked fiddle breakdowns and honky-tonk weepers — it wasn't a city audience either, at least not the sort that Bob Wills and Milton Brown had stirred with their jazz licks and hot rhythms. No, by 1970 the people who bought the bulk of Music City's product came from that vast modern American territory which is neither city nor country: suburbia. The Nashville sound had transmogrified country music into Suburban and Western. Unfortunately, as the music became more formulaic and mass-produced, country songwriters sank gradually to the status of Tin Pan Alley hacks, turning out hit after lucrative hit according to pattern.

The rise of songwriters as an artistic force in their own right, as exemplified especially by the Tootsie's crowd, helped change all that. It was a core of writers who formed the nucleus of both the Austin "progressive country" singers and the "Nashville outlaws" of the 1970s, the two groups that did more than anyone else to rescue country music from its near-terminal blandness. These rebels shared a strong antipathy to the inane lyrics and musical monotony which had come to mark the industry's commercial product.

The Tootsie's crowd, the Nashville outlaws, and the Austin singer/songwriters all sought to redeem, in one form or another, true "country" music from commercial adulteration. They found a public television show in Austin, that nexus of hippies and rednecks, offering them a soapbox with a national reach. The best of the Austin "folk-rock" songwriters, such as Fromholz, Clark, Van Zandt, Murphey, Walker, and Bridger, had early on found ACL a friendly venue. With Willie Nelson's continuing benign influence, so eventually did most of Nashville's rebellious and creative country-western composers. Kris Kristofferson, Billy Joe Shaver, Tompall Glaser, Mel Tillis, Roger Miller, Moe Bandy, Hoyt Axton, even the Mysterious Rhinestone Cowboy himself, David Allan Coe, eventually journeyed to Austin to tape their work.

"Songwriters editions" have over the years provided some of the most important avenues for these artists. An encore to the blockbuster "Songwriters Special" by Willie and friends followed in season six with the same musicians. In the eighth season (1983) a younger generation of writers received the chance to display their talents. In a "Songwriters Showcase," Rodney Crowell, John Prine, Guy Clark, Keith Sykes, Bill Caswell, and Rosanne Cash, a group of writers often identified with the "new" Nashville, played guitars and traded songs in the same kind of easy, chatty environment that showed the Tootsie's crowd to advantage.

That season also included a "West Texas Songwriters Special" featuring Butch Hancock, Jimmie Gilmore, David Halley, and Townes Van Zandt, accompanied by Spider Johnson on the musical saw. West Texas has been known as a musical motherlode ever since Bob Wills grew up near the little town of Turkey. Waylon Jennings, Buddy Holly, Joe Ely, Terry Allen, and the Maines Brothers Band, to mention only a few of the region's products, all hailed from the Lubbock area. In honor of this occasion, the ACL staff graced the set with a hay bale and a stretch of barbed-wire fence.

In seasons nine and ten Freddie Powers hosted two songwriters shows. On the first, a bearded Merle Haggard and Willie Nelson joined him, and the three traded solos, duets, and trios. The concert turned into an impromptu tribute to Floyd Tillman, present in the audience, whose melodic complexities and popular lyrics had influenced both Nelson and Haggard. "Pure magic," judged Darrell Royal. "Pure magic." The following year Powers brought back Haggard and Nelson and expanded the circle to include Whitey Shafer and Spud Goodall in a program that crossed the borders between country and jazz. But if Willie Nelson is a

country music Shakespeare, he's also an old hay-baler; the close-up work of the camera in these intimate specials remains a fine character study of this complex poet-farmer-musician. In the eleventh season Merle Haggard repaid Freddie Powers' hospitality by inviting him to be a special guest on his own Austin City Limits show — his third.

As its attention to songwriters evolved into conscious commitment, Austin City Limits concentrated on presenting a full spectrum of contemporary writers. Season eleven, for example, brought a Women Songwriters Special, with Rosanne Cash, Lacy J. Dalton, Emmylou Harris, Gail Davies, Pam Rose, and Mary Ann Kennedy. The themes and attitudes that interest the new woman singer/songwriter suggest an exciting trend in contemporary country music, full of implications for the future of what has been, after all, predominantly masculine terrain.

Once again, in the eighties, a generation of singer/songwriters was making waves in country music, and the young men and women who played the ACL songwriters shows belonged to the vanguard. They were creating a clear alternative to the Nashville sound. Many of them knew the recording studios of New York and Los Angeles as well as those of Nashville. They could draw on rock, rhythm and blues, and old-time country for their material. And in a curious resurrection of the term, the newspapers occasionally labeled them, too, "progressive country."

N OT SURPRISINGLY, ACL's success attracted problems of its own. One of them concerned the studio audiences on which so much of the show's liveliness depended. As Austin City Limits grew more popular and attracted more big-name stars, the tapings became a powerful drawing card in Austin. Gone were the days when the staff had to put in a hasty call to Joe Gracey to unload a few more tickets. Now you had to be lucky to get them, since they usually disappeared within a few minutes of becoming available at KLRU studios, grabbed up by fans, some of whom had been waiting since the crack of dawn. The supply, too, had shrunk over the years, for several reasons.

One of those was internal. Station management had discovered that ACL tickets made an important power tool useful in fundraising and repaying favors. It therefore kept a sizable bloc under control, which never went up for grabs.

Another reason had nothing to do with the station, but came from outside. An incident in the seventh season precipitated the events. Kris Kristofferson, indisputably one of the original "Nashville outlaws," had agreed to play.

Kristofferson's booking itself typified the maneuvering so often necessary when it came to matching big stars to a small budget. Lickona had sought Kris for some time, but, as in Loretta Lynn's case, could not get past the star's manager. Finally he cornered the singer backstage at a concert and popped the question directly. "Sure," said Kris, "I've always wanted to be on that show. Why didn't you ask me before?" His manager, as it happened, had not thought it financially worthwhile to forward the invitations.

But finally here was Kristofferson poised to play and 700 eager fans poised to listen. Then, just as the band was ready to hit the stage, an unlucky rat used its body to close two electrical circuits somewhere in the maze of university wiring. The campus fell into a darkness that, in the windowless Studio 6A, was utter. The crowd could do nothing but sit helplessly in the cavern, sing a few choruses of "London Homesick Blues," then file gropingly down the stairs and out into a driving rain. Electricians solved the problem the next day. Kristofferson returned and did a fine show; but repercussions followed.

The local fire marshal, browsing in his morning paper, was appalled to read about those 700 people in the studio. He immediately put the university on notice to cut the audiences to 250. The decision brought pleasure to no one. To create the illusion of a full house, the ACL crew had to pull in the bleachers and be careful with their cameras. Even so, 250 people do not have the energy and presence of 700. Moreover, the reduction meant that an even higher proportion of the audience consisted of people who had acquired their tickets through executive largesse rather than by competing for them with a crowd of aficionados. As a result, audiences began more frequently to contain "dead spots" composed of people uninformed and less than wild about the music onstage. Their presence not only tended sometimes to create the proverbial wet-blanket effect, but reduced the number of shot options available to the camera crew. You don't, after all, want deadpan faces on your television show. A diminished

Kris Kristofferson

audience capacity also angered many ACL regulars who found themselves shut out of the studio. A flurry of letters descended on local newspapers.

Eventually, with the help of a member of the university's Board of Regents, the station got the studio modified to legally qualify 450 people. Still, in the minds of ACL staff who remember the large and diverse audiences that used to be assured by plentiful seats and tickets, that is not enough. Arhos and Lickona agree. "The distribution of tickets remains our thorniest problem," says Lickona, lamenting that U.T. students and staff usually snatch up the few available tickets before the larger Austin population can get to them.

Nevertheless, the tapings remain wonderful for those clever or lucky enough to get in. "I like the spirit in the studio when a performance takes off," declared Mary-Margaret Byerman, who became a faithful fan upon moving to Austin with her husband, Keith, when he accepted an assistant professor's job in the university's English department. "It's the most intimate situation I've ever been in with a performer, and it's never been repeated anywhere else except at Emmajoe's or the Alamo Lounge — two Austin clubs now dead. The only bad shows are those where the performer thinks he's in a recording studio instead of doing a concert, and repeats songs. . . . There aren't many like that, though. I go regularly for the electricity of the performance; it's great entertainment."

One problem perhaps inevitable with the increasing national prominence of Austin City Limits is the selection of talent in accordance with a more national common denominator of taste. Along with performers like Willie Nelson, Merle Haggard, Ray Charles, or Kris Kristofferson, who retain impeccable country and soul credentials despite their mass popularity, the series has booked a number of what are generally called "Nashville-pop" artists (or, in Joe Gracey's harsher term, "Gnashville-slick"). ACL's choice of such acts as Mickey Gilley and his Urban Cowboys, T. G. Sheppard, Tammy Wynette, Dottie West, Juice Newton, Eddie Rabbitt, Eddy Raven, Lee Greenwood, the Oak Ridge Boys, and other groups as comfortable on *Billboard*'s pop charts as on its country charts, has dismayed watchers interested in country roots, regional music, or just "authenticity." A letter Bill Arhos received in 1983 from a Missouri viewer praised the show's "early enterprise and the opportunity to enjoy new talent, new sounds, fresh ideas from young and often unknown performers, and an occasional look back to our mountain and frontier musical heritage."

Then it segued into an elegiac mode. "Where has it gone?" the writer asked. "Over the past couple of seasons, the upgrading of sets and lighting have become a polished backdrop to a string of commercially successful stars and, now, recycled American Bandstand favorites trying to hold their age as well as Dick Clark.

"Does this mean there are no more Cajun fiddlers, contemporary Mexican bands, John Hartfords or Lost Gonzos to be found and developed? Or is it that Austin City Limits has fallen victim to commercial television's reluctance to risk much on the unknown? I hope not."

The writer spoke for many longtime viewers worried about what might be happening to a favorite show. Arhos wrote back, acknowledging ACL's new polish and laying much of the blame at the feet of "system pressure." By 1983 ACL had finally achieved a prime-time release slot from PBS. While this meant that over 250 stations were buying the series and showing it to six million viewers, it also meant that station managers were more aware of its content than ever before. They were anxious about how that content would play to a prime-time audience. Furthermore, record companies and talent agencies, keenly aware of those audience numbers, constantly agitated to get their own artists in the klieg lights. Austin City Limits had become big-time.

Another factor working against a no-holds-barred selection of talent was, ironically, Arhos' success in getting the show "simulcast" on country music radio stations. Simulcasting—broadcasting the audio track over the radio simultaneously with the video telecast—began in 1979. As long as the simulcasting stations pitched themselves to a "progressive" audience, as did for instance Austin's KUT-FM, there was no problem: Listeners tolerated, even appreciated, innovative programming. But as more mainstream "commercial country" stations picked up the show, complications arose. A program director with a tight country playlist didn't want to hear somebody like George Thorogood and the Destroyers or Bonnie Raitt blowing away his safe package of Top Forty tunes and scaring away advertisers.

Indeed, at least one station manager pulled the plug on Joe "King" Carrasco's simulcast in season six and fired off an angry letter to Arhos. Carrasco's rollicking blend of Tex-Mex, rock and roll, and Nuevo Wavo was not country, he said—an assessment with which Carrasco would certainly agree. Thus, oddly enough, a highly successful venture of noncommercial public television found its freedom curtailed by the narrow requirements of American commercial radio, which former KSAN-FM deejay Bob Simmons, among others, has blasted as a "barren monoculture."

While naturally pleased by the show's success, Lickona admits to some sensitivity regarding these charges. Acknowledging that national programming concerns have indeed motivated a tendency to book middle-

of-the-road acts, he defends such booking on grounds that big pop acts attract more viewers, who then stick around for lesser-known entertainers. Austin singer and songwriter Nanci Griffith, for example, made her debut before a national television audience on a program headlined by the Gatlin Brothers (who years previously had made *their* national TV debut on ACL). No one would deny that the exposure helped Griffith's career. One might also remember, in defense of relatively mass programming, that ever since the Nixon administration slashed public television funds, "educational" television, to support itself, has been forced to become more and more of an entertainment industry in the mold of its private sector competitors.

At the same time, Lickona stubbornly resists pressure to further increase the ratio of country-pop acts. Even in recent years, in the midst of a popularity that enables it to pick and choose, ACL has continued to showcase locally based bands. Some of these indeed were at the time already poised on the brink of national prominence, such as Stevie Ray Vaughan and Double Trouble or the Fabulous Thunderbirds, two of the country's finest blues bands, or rocker Joe Ely. But others were purely hometown acts such as Austin's popular Beto y los Fairlanes or Eric Johnson, a legendary but largely unrecorded local guitarist. Johnson, a jazz virtuoso, included a country-flavored medley of tunes, but there was no disguising the stark fact that he belonged neither to country nor to pop. Still, fans mobbed the stage at his performance, and letters poured in praising his work.

In fact, the proliferation of country-pop acts on ACL reflected the state of country music itself. Controversy over the distinction between "real" and "commercial" country music has existed at least since the early seventies, when crossover mania hit the industry with a vengeance. Singers

such as Tammy Wynette, Barbara Mandrell, Olivia Newton-John, John Denver, and Kenny Rogers were being packaged and sold as "country" even though their work bore no discernible historical or cultural relationship to what had traditionally been known as country music. Actually, they purveyed middle-of-the-road material that had more in common with Doris Day or Perry Como than Grandpa Jones or the Skillet Lickers. But Nashville is a place where the bottom line means everything, and the new country-pop fusion met undeniable success in the marketplace. The Country Music Association bestowed its approval on the popular sound in the form of various awards, and only a few disgruntled purists complained.

Unarguably, entertainers like T. G. Sheppard, B. J. Thomas, Janie Fricke, Juice Newton, Eddy Raven, Eddie Rabbitt, and Lee Greenwood represent a distinctive category of contemporary music, a commercial hybrid that, however labeled, has sold millions of records. And these records have aired primarily on radio stations that consider themselves "country." Austin City Limits has presented concerts by all of these musicians, and Tammy Wynette, too; Wynette and Rabbitt's show won the highest ratings in the series' history. Yet it was quite a contrast to tune in one week and catch the pure honky-tonk sounds of George Strait, the San Marcos ranch foreman turned country singer, and another week to find Lee Greenwood crooning his syrupy popular ballads. Greenwood, the CMA's 1983 Male Singer of the Year, delivered an unabashedly sentimental performance, going so far as to haul a reluctant little girl out of the bleachers to sit embarrassed on the stage while he addressed to her a mawkish number called "I Owe You." One notable critic snorted that it was the lowest point in ACL's history. Nevertheless, both studio and television audiences seemed to approve. As Larry Gatlin said about country-pop in another context, "Producers are just trying to cut hit records. . . . if that's what America is buying, maybe there isn't much choice" (*Country Music,* July/August 1984).

As long as it continued a major force in the Nashville music business, country-pop would have its place on Austin City Limits. But as the eighties marched on, the country-pop phenomenon seemed to lose momentum and begin its decline. By 1985, critic Robert Palmer could announce in the *New York Times* that the Nashville sound had had its day. Figures showed that record sales by stars like Tammy Wynette and Conway Twitty were down by half from their late 1970s peak. The Nashville sound's audience had aged, moving on into their fifties, and the youngsters who might have renewed it sought their music elsewhere. Interestingly, the new generation of country music listeners were turning back to the leaner, purer style that characterized the music before the Nashville producers injected it with orchestral arrangements and sentimentality. While country-pop performers appeared to be losing ground, the "new traditionalists" such as Ricky Skaggs, George Strait, the Judds, the Whites, John Anderson, and Dwight Yoakam found their popularity increasing steadily. A new trend seemed to be in the making.

Evidence of renewed respect for country music's roots and power might also be found in Neil Young's tenth-season ACL performance. In a kind of reverse crossover, Young, whose work with Crosby, Stills, and Nash, with Crazy Horse, and on his own had earned him a reputation as a seminal rock musician of the sixties, decided to abandon the music that made him famous in order to play "traditional" country—"even more traditional," he said, than that of Merle and Waylon. Playing with a full country band called the Interna-

tional Harvesters, including a pedal steel guitar and the authoritative Cajun fiddle of Rufus Thibodeaux, he sounded thoroughly convincing, even with a cowboy hat on his head. Afterward he praised the production.

"I like this show," he told Dallas writer Bryan Woolley. "This is a good musician's show. This is about music, it's not about images. It's not rock 'n' roll. I like it for that. There's no bullshit. There's no pizzazz, no crap. I can't handle production numbers." Paul Bosner would have beamed.

Actually, the national appetite for good material probably exceeds the ability of any single musical category to satiate it. Still, Lickona points out that the show hasn't gone so far as to include heavy metal or punk-rock or fusion jazz in its potpourri. Nor, at least at the date of this writing, has it hosted Kenny Rogers or Barbara Mandrell. Though it may suffer pangs of MOR in the interest of balance, the series tries to stay anchored to "roots music," in Lickona's phrase, whether that be country, blues, or jazz.

Although it is more difficult to go against the grain than it used to be, room remains on ACL for the experimental and the off-beat. The show provided one of the first national audiences for the iconoclastic "country-punk" band Rank and File, for instance. Joe Ely, another partisan of the unorthodox, was invited not once, but twice. The second shot came in the tenth season. In the five years since his first appearance, however, his music had evolved from the loping West Texas rhythms he'd first brought to Austin. Some KLRU staff members, apparently not *au courant* with this evolution, were pained and shocked by the hard-edged rock his band now hurled into the night at ear-piercing volume. Moreover, since the taping occurred on Halloween— traditionally a weird night in Austin—outrageous costumes distinguished a large number of his fans. But while the show was recorded on

Halloween, it did not air on Halloween, an anachronism that created a degree of annoyance among PBS station managers who found themselves hard pressed to explain the costumes. Whether Ely will draw a third invitation remains to be seen.

Blues-rocker George Thorogood and the Destroyers were another unusual band who somehow slipped into Studio 6A. They soon had the audience gyrating like victims of St. Vitus. "The most disgusting show I've ever seen," said one disenchanted KLRU executive; but the under-thirty audience gave it an A+. Thoro-

SEASON 6
1981

601	The Charlie Daniels Band
602	Bobby Bare Lacy J. Dalton
603	George Jones with Hank Thompson
604	Ray Price Asleep at the Wheel
605	Johnny Rodriguez Alabama
606	David Grisman Quintet "Mandolin Special" with Tiny Moore, Jethro Burns, and Johnny Gimble
607	Bill Monroe & Bluegrass Boys Riders in the Sky
608	Tony Joe White Gary Stewart
609	Songwriters Encore Willie Nelson Floyd Tillman Hank Cochran Sonny Throckmorton Red Lane Whitey Shafer
610	Charley Pride Razzy Bailey
611	Michael Murphey Ed Bruce
612	Leo Kottke Passenger
613	Joe "King" Carrasco The Sir Douglas Quintet

good's tape went on the air with a concert by David Olney and the X-Rays, another band not likely to win any CMA awards.

It was a risk, too, some felt, to bring in Bonnie Raitt, known for her hard-rocking and gutsy blues style. Risk or no, it paid off handsomely. Raitt's intense guitar work and powerful vocals won over audience and crew alike. Her performance radiated more real "country" feeling than did those of many more famous stars. The show turned into a barn-burner when Austin's LeRoi Brothers and the Fabulous Thunderbirds' Kim Wilson joined Raitt in toe-to-toe blues jamming. As if that weren't enough, the blues musicians invited legendary rockabilly stars Sleepy LaBeef and Ray Campi to share the bill. The sight of Austin's own Ray Campi frantically slapping and clambering over his stand-up string bass may have been a television first.

Other gambles did not entirely succeed. Jimmy Buffett, for example, who had appeared in the second season, recorded an hour-long show in the ninth. It was too long. While he delivered a catchy brand of pop-rock spiced with tropical rhythms, like a snow-cone it ran to slush after an hour. Similarly with Charlie Daniels: A half-hour was fine, but his one-hour boogie show in season six would have numbed a camel, as one observer phrased it. On the other hand, B. B. King's long show was a stunning success. King rehearsed his performance in the afternoon, then played it note for note and joke for joke that evening without losing an iota of apparent spontaneity. Though the blues great might seem an unlikely choice for a "country" series, he kept at least some members of his audience enthralled for the length of his rehearsal, then another ninety minutes that night, and again sixty minutes more when the tape played; and they would happily have repeated the entire experience. King's power

perhaps stems from the truth that his music, like early white country music, embodies the genuine and deeply felt emotional experience of a living "folk" culture. (The American anthropologist Edward Sapir often pointedly contrasted the "authentic" culture of grass-roots American life, as found in autonomous and close-knit rural black, white, and Native American communities, with the "spurious" so-called high culture imported from Europe by our intellectuals.)

The Pete Fountain show was another experiment that worked. Again Johnny Gimble took a hand in it. Pete Fountain had long admired Austin City Limits, often watching it in the dressing room at his New Orleans club. His friend Gimble suggested that he do the show himself, and so Fountain found himself blowing his gold clarinet in Studio 6A. Wearing a big cowboy hat, he opened with a jazz rendition of "Walking the Floor over You," then pulled Gimble into the act. Gimble, at first tentative, soon got into the swing of things. Television viewers leaped from their armchairs and danced around the room. The tape later became part of a jazz special. Watchers raised eyebrows, seeing one of country music's most noted fiddle players on stage with Dixieland's most prominent clarinetist. But to work for Bob Wills, as Gimble had done, a musician had to be able to play more than country. And besides, as Willie Nelson once allowed, "Hell, Gimble always did play jazz, he just calls it country." Not least important, the duets by Fountain and Gimble eloquently suggested the amalgam of styles that lay at the heart of early Texas swing.

Larry Gatlin's comment on country pop is from an interview with Kip Kirby, *Country Music,* July/August 1984, pp. 27–30. Neil Young was quoted by Bryan Woolley, "Neil Young Goes Country All the Way," *Dial,* January 1985.

B. B. King

Sound: David Hough, Billy Lee Myers

Cameramen: *left to right, standing,* Mike Archenhold, Robert Moorehead, Vance Holmes, director Gary Menotti, Doug Robb; *kneeling,* Michael Emery, technical director Ed Fuentes

Bill Arhos, Terry Lickona, Gary Menotti, Doug Robb

Lighting: Bob Selby, Walter Olden

Associate producers: Jeff Peterson, Susie Caldwell

Makeup: Estreya Kesler

Video technicians: Dan Martaus, Bink Williams

BY THE TIME ALLAN MUIR swung into his second season as director in 1980–1981, the Austin City Limits production crew had forged themselves into a well-oiled unit, or perhaps more accurately, into a family. Five years working together had given David Hough, Bob Selby, Gary Menotti, Mike Archenhold, Dean Rabourn, and Bink Williams a combat veteran's sense of camaraderie and mutual dependence. They had weathered start-up vagaries, internal bickering, and several stand-offs with station management over wages and equipment. They had learned much since the show's inception; in fact they had emerged into seasoned professionals who could hold their own in any network organization. And indeed they received offers; but Austin was a hard place to leave. Each year they returned to ACL and public television's low wages. If they couldn't make a lot of money, at least they could have a lot of fun.

Allan Muir retained much of the "national look" that Clark Santee had instilled into the show. Though he toned down the colored gels and the star filters, he continued to direct the cameras' attention to the stage much more than to the audience. Selby's lighting effects followed suit: Whereas in Bosner's era the entire studio was lit "white," with no distinction between stage and bleachers, the lighting had by now evolved so that the audience was almost in the dark and the performer in the limelight. The concept of concert as "participatory event," for which the audience-in-the-round mattered as much as the entertainer, had essentially evaporated. "The performer was getting lost in the crowd," Gary Menotti would say, explaining the change. This did not mean that Muir was uninterested in concert dynamics. On the contrary, it remained his overriding mission to transmit as much of the musical energy of a live performance to the television audience as possible. But he had a different directoral style: Muir believed that focusing on the performance act itself most effectively drew the television viewer into the music.

Muir said to Scott Busby, a writer for the Austin magazine *Third Coast,* "I like doing music on television because I have as much fun as the musician does. I just love orchestrating and making everything melt together — making the television performance as good as the musician's performance."

Muir commuted between Austin and his home and family in Los Angeles. Though he very much enjoyed doing Austin City Limits, the strain of the commute led him to leave the show after two and a half seasons. He bestowed the director's mantle upon his associate Gary Menotti. Menotti had begun his ACL career "pulling cables" for the camera crane — virtually the lowliest job on the crew — then moved on to work as camera operator and stage manager before becoming Muir's associate director. He thus obtained invaluable knowledge of the show's inner workings. Taking over near the end of the seventh season, Menotti retained the style he had absorbed from Muir, refining it according to his own lights. He remains performer-oriented, preferring to cut to the audience only when an integral relationship clearly exists between their response and the music. In season eight the station added a hand-held camera to the three studio cameras and the crane camera. The hand-held gives Menotti more flexibility in close-ups and shots from unusual angles, which he uses to advantage in exploring stage dynamics. The show thus continues to evolve along lines of close attention to music and musicians, on an increasingly professional level. Partisans of the early look sometimes criticize it as "overproduced." In any case, the old Austin funkiness that marked its infancy has largely disappeared, replaced by a lush style that totally bespeaks the eighties.

Season seven also brought another set refinement: the adoption of the show's trademark skyline view of Austin as a backdrop. Lickona conceived the idea but Augie Kymmel, who had first translated Scafe's and Bosner's concepts into wood, accomplished the design and construction. Typical landmarks stand out in the tableau: the Capitol, the university tower, the new downtown buildings (the set has to be revised periodically to keep abreast of Austin's growth). Up close, the thing bristles with wires and Christmas tree lights like a Rube Goldberg contraption; but backlit, with potted plants strategically located, it effectively suggests the Austin skyline on a summer night. Menotti plays heavily on this effect, directing his camera crew to shoot through the leaves, framing the set so as to suggest the open sky. Trying to capture the point of view of a listener at an outdoor concert, he wants the scene to seem bathed in moonlight. Between Menotti's direction and Bob Selby's lighting, the effort has been remarkably successful. Tourists are continually surprised to learn the city has no outdoor concert site where ACL is shot.

By the time the seventh season rolled around, political tides at the station had shifted again. Bill Arhos returned to the show as executive producer, where he remains. At the same time, Lickona left the KLRU payroll, becoming an independent producer; eventually the core of the ACL staff followed him. Organized as an independent production company, they now contract with the station to produce the show. This arrangement has proved efficient and productive.

Following on the wide popularity of the regular series, a demand arose for country music "specials" that PBS stations could use in fundraising drives. These spin-offs have won laurels of their own. The first one, "Down Home Country Music," a three-hour program, showcased traditional and contemporary country performers, all of whom had previously appeared in ACL productions. Arhos served as executive producer, Lickona as producer, and Muir and Menotti as co-directors. The special captured a Gold Award as "Best Network Music Program" in the 1982 International Film and Television Festival of New York.

"Down Home" was succeeded by "Country Music Jubilee," a special hosted by Jerry Reed which drew on ACL film clips. Al Green and Cynthia Clawson hosted another major production, a two-hour gospel special called "I'll Fly Away." In 1984 Arhos and associate producer/director Carol Patton Cornsilk flew to Nashville. Working at the Cannery studios with a Nashville Network truck and crew, they shot a special titled "Legends of Country Music," produced and directed by *Hee Haw*'s Bob Boatman. Hosted by Hoyt Axton, "The Legends" featured many of the same musicians who had appeared on ACL's regular season "Country Legends" show. The special won a Bronze Award in the 1985 New York International Film Festival. Two "Country Classics" compilations consisted of clips, edited by Arhos, Scafe, and Vaughn, from regular season shows. Willie Nelson hosted "Country Memories," another clip show. A special titled "Good Rockin'" starred a trin-

SEASON 7
1982

701 Emmylou Harris
Rodney Crowell

702 Kris Kristofferson

703 Jerry Reed
Chet Atkins

704 Johnny Lee
Charly McClain

705 Willie Nelson
Guy Clark

706 The Merle Haggard Show

707 The Bellamy Brothers
John Anderson

708 Larry Gatlin
Ricky Skaggs

709 Tompall & Glaser Brothers
George Strait

710 Don McLean
Terri Gibbs

711 Roy Clark
The Geezinslaws

712 Pete Fountain
Jazzmanian Devil

713 George Thorogood &
The Destroyers
David Olney & The X-Rays

Terry Lickona, Gary Menotti, Bill Arhos, Todd Abrams (vice president of Budweiser advertising), Jerry Lee Lewis (seated)

several records. In addition to those by Earl Scruggs, the Nashville Super Pickers, and the Texas Playboys, Carl Perkins issued a record called *Live at Austin City Limits* on Blue Suede Records, and Roy Clark released his ACL performance on Churchill Records. It stayed on the charts longer than any of his other recordings. Steve Goodman excerpted a few cuts from his ACL audio track for an album, and Gary P. Nunn's show, including of course "London Homesick Blues," became available as *Home with the Armadillo.*

Various forms of Austin City Limits memorabilia such as belt buckles, gimme caps, and lapel pins have taken their place as twentieth-century Americana; so have, inevitably, T-shirts. ACL T-shirts sell by the thousands across the country. Arhos trots out snapshots of ACL T-shirt wearers framed by the Acropolis and the Great Pyramid. One Columbia, South Carolina, bowling team named itself Austin City Limits, with T-shirts to prove it.

Beginning in 1975, when Howard Chalmers first pitched the idea to the company, Lone Star Beer was associated with Austin City Limits, first as free beer supplier, than as underwriter. After eight years, however, a business merger compelled Lone Star to drop its financial support. Since the ninth season Anheuser-Busch and Budweiser Beer have filled the breach, underwriting the show and pouring free beer for studio audiences. In 1985 Budweiser funded ACL to the tune of about $133,000, almost one-fourth the total budget.

Contributions like those of Budweiser are essential to the show's survival, at least in its present form. Even with them, each new season means another struggle for money, not only for salaries but for maintenance and repairs. New equipment is virtually an impossible dream. A public television station's budget does not permit the regular replacement of

ity of fifties rockabilly legends: Roy Orbison, Jerry Lee Lewis, and Carl Perkins.

Willie Nelson, not surprisingly, was the prime mover behind another landmark project called "Swingin' over the Rainbow." "Swingin'" featured Willie and band and assorted compatriots like Johnny Gimble and jazz guitarist Jackie King. Ray Benson of Asleep at the Wheel talked Willie into organizing the show, and Lone Star Beer underwrote it. The special paid tribute to Django Reinhardt and the late thirties "hot jazz" that so strongly influenced Willie's generation. But it also honored Western Swing guitarists Zeke Campbell and Eldon Shamblin, whose single-string jazz runs and subtle chordings were making history before anybody had

heard of Django or Charlie Christian. Musically very important, the special proved a fund-raising blockbuster also, generating $850,000 in one day alone.

Austin City Limits even appeared on commercial television, in the form of a series entitled *Austin City Limits Encore.* The editing necessary for commercial breaks detracted, of course, from the concert atmosphere of the original, but Arhos was glad to make the sale. If he and PBS executives could figure out the byzantine copyright and royalty ramifications, they would like to sell videocassettes, too. No one foresaw the new video technology and its revenue possibilities in ACL's early days, so contracts did not make appropriate provisions.

The show naturally has spawned

worn-out and obsolete equipment. KLRU still uses its 1974 state-of-the-art cameras and consoles, although by industry standards they have become certified antiques, years out of date. The studio cameras seem held together by dint of baling wire, chewing gum, and the engineering genius of Gene Harris and Jack Wells. Whereas new computerized cameras can be adjusted in about forty-five seconds, these still take four worker-hours to set up. But at approximately $150,000 apiece for new ones, the situation is not likely to improve soon. The recognizably superior color quality of Austin City Limits excites marvel among visiting engineers when they see the equipment.

Conditions are no better when it comes to sound and light. The heart of David Hough's bailiwick is a sixteen-track audio board designed for monaural sound. The audience mikes and a time-coding device take up four tracks. This leaves twelve tracks for mixing the band's sound; and in these days of sophisticated electronics there may be many more inputs than that onstage. A modern board would have a minimum of twenty-four tracks to work with, more likely thirty-six, forty-eight, or even sixty. With only twelve tracks, Hough must resort to various kinds of ingenious "cheating" to record a full range of stereophonic sound. The lighting console, too, has outlived its day. If Selby possessed updated equipment, not only could he produce a wider range of effects but, for example, he could change the lighting during a show, a desirable option. New audio and lighting equipment, however, would cost a quarter of a million. It's no wonder that the backstage humor is sometimes bordered in black or that the crew takes a kind of perverse and defiant pride in their success at battling adverse conditions.

Editing procedures, on the other hand, have markedly improved over the years. After the less than happy results of the Nashville editing sessions in season four, the series embraced "double-system editing" geographically as well as mechanically. For a couple of years Allan Muir took the video to Los Angeles for editing, while the audio track stayed in Austin for post-production "sweetening." Finally KLRU obtained CMX editing machines of its own, a great step forward. Then, with the advent of time-coding and VCR, "off-line editing" became possible, and the long nights and tribulations of Bruce Scafe's time became a thing of the past. In the off-line process, Lickona and associate producer Susan Caldwell review the rough tape on an ordinary television monitor; they can even do this at home. Thanks to time-coding, whereby each frame of the tape is numbered to the tenth of a second, they can then plot ideas about cuts and sequences with great precision. Finally, armed with notes taken during these sessions, Lickona and Menotti take the tape to the computerized machines and electronically perform the final editing.

But behind all the swirl of economic and technical details is the music. The music is what supplies the energy that turns the wheels. It's the message and the medium too; and the wonder is that so much of it pours through that 21-inch glow in the living room. In the television concert as art form, performers, live audience, producers and directors, camera and sound crews, finally even television spectators all play essential parts. In this case, their orchestrated efforts have fostered an electronic flowering of grass-roots music reminiscent of the early radio barn dances. Indeed, one might well describe Austin City Limits as the Marshall McLuhan generation's own barn dance.

Allan Muir is quoted by Scott Busby, "Bright Lights, City Limits," *Third Coast*, January 1982, pp. 32–35.

**SEASON 8
1983**

801 **Mickey Gilley
T. G. Sheppard**
802 **Don Williams
West Texas Songwriters Special**
803 **Roy Orbison**
804 **Songwriters Showcase with Rodney Crowell, John Prine & Friends**
805 **B. B. King**
806 **Janie Fricke
B. J. Thomas**
807 **Frizzell & West
Con Hunley**
808 **Michael Murphey
Gary P. Nunn**
809 **Rosanne Cash
Steve Wariner**
810 **Rank & File
Delbert McClinton**
811 **Tammy Wynette
John Conlee**
812 **Roger Miller
Earl Thomas Conley**
813 **Loretta Lynn**

A TEN-YEAR-OLD TELEVISION PROGRAM has reached a ripe old age. Austin City Limits is now steaming into its second decade. But if the years have altered its appearance, it retains a remarkably youthful feel, thanks primarily to its high-spirited staff and the lively music itself. The face of Austin, whose fortunes have intertwined significantly with those of ACL, has changed more noticeably than the program's. The city has exploded into a boomtown with double its 1974 population. As one of Austin's most visible and attractive products, Austin City Limits must accept its share of praise or blame for this development.

From the very beginning the show's lead-ins — the image sequences leading to the introduction of the featured performer — cast Austin in a light worthy of a tourist brochure. Since then, as if mirroring the transformation of the city, the lead-ins have evolved from Bosner's early string of nightclub shots to a slick montage of scenic vignettes. Those of the second and third seasons portrayed Austin as a musician's mecca, depicting guitarists flocking into town on planes, buses, and pickups. Over the action, radio KVET deejay and Geezinslaw Brothers member Sammy Allred intoned: "I understand they're comin' in from deep in the heart o' Texas to do some pickin'." An antique Greyhound bus belonging to Alvin Crow and the Pleasant Valley Boys figured prominently in the footage. The camera panned the bus as it cruised into town, then cut to the interior where Alvin and the band were happily sawing away at a Bob Wills tune. Turning to the band, Alvin drawled, "Time to pack 'em up, boys, we're comin' into Austin," whereupon the scene shifted to Studio 6A and the evening's performance.

As the series wore on, the lead-ins highlighted other aspects of the Austin environment: its green rolling hills, the inviting waters of Barton Springs, crystal-clear streams, beautifully framed shots of cactus and sunsets and rock formations. The city's association with a youthful "lifestyle" was reinforced in shots of attractive, wholesome young people participating in armadillo races, street fairs, chili cook-offs, boisterous pickup rides, and similarly picturesque pleasures. It was a Chamber of Commerce president's publicity dream come true. It brought results, too: Thousands of immigrants followed the spoor of the good life to Austin.

This effect of the show does not make Bill Arhos particularly happy, despite accolades by the downtown business establishment. Sourly noting the advent of traffic congestion, air pollution, and sky-rocketing rents in what Doug Sahm had called "Groover's Paradise," Arhos likes to wish aloud that they had named the series something else: "Pasadena City Limits," maybe, "Newark City Limits" — anything but Austin.

Ironically, Austin's own music scene nearly fell victim to the boomtown prosperity it helped fuel. Club after club — nearly every one that appeared in Bosner's first lead-in — succumbed to rising rents and the real estate squeeze. Soap Creek Saloon, Antone's, the Alliance Wagonyard, the Split Rail, Castle Creek, the Silver Dollar, even the hallowed Skyline Club, where both Hank Williams and Johnny Horton are said to have played their last dates, all had to close

SEASON 9
1984

901 Ray Charles
     Lee Greenwood

902 Jerry Lee Lewis

903 Freddie Powers with
     Willie Nelson &
     Merle Haggard

904 Gary Morris
     Gail Davies

905 The Whites
     New Grass Revival

906 Jimmy Buffett

907 Johnny Rodriguez
     David Allan Coe

908 Dottie West
     Floyd Cramer

909 Bonnie Raitt
     The Le Roi Brothers with
     Ray Campi & Sleepy
     La Beef

910 John Anderson
     Lisa Gilkyson

911 George Strait
     The Kendalls

912 Country Legends:
     Kitty Wells, Pee Wee King,
     Faron Young, Joe Maphis,
     Sons of the Pioneers

913 Stevie Ray Vaughan
     & Double Trouble
     The Fabulous Thunderbirds

or move to less desirable locations. To view those early ACL lead-ins is to glimpse a lost Austin. No more perfect symbol of the city's metamorphosis exists than the high-rise office building now standing where Armadillo World Headquarters once hosted Willie Nelson, Freddy King, Commander Cody, and a disproportionately high percentage of the nation's leading musicians. The Armadillo closed its doors for good on January 1, 1980; the chief tenant of the new high-rise is IBM.

When the Armadillo opened in 1970, its identification with the hardshelled little mammal from which it took its name puzzled many oldtimers. After all, for generations the shy burrower had been little more than a varmint that annoyed ranchers and possessed a penchant for getting run over on highways. Nevertheless, despite all attempts to stamp it out, the critter flourished in its harsh surroundings. In the 1960s, U.T. cartoonist Glenn Whitehead adopted the animal as a motif in the campus humor magazine. Later, attracted by its subterranean and vaguely subversive survival qualities, AWHQ resident artist Jim Franklin took up the armadillo and made it the star of his paintings and posters. His fellow poster artists Michael Priest, Guy Juke, and Ken Featherstone adopted the beast as well, and it became a central totem of the Austin mystique. Having survived as an animal, it now proliferated as an image. In 1985, with Austin's flagship concert hall five years gone, the phone directory listed at least fifteen businesses with "Armadillo" in their names, from Armadillo Air to Armadillo Wrecker. Not only that, but the Texas Sesquicentennial of 1986, marking the 150th anniversary of Texas' independence from Mexico, chose for its official mascot the armadillo (wearing, of course, a cowboy hat). The apotheosis of the humble creature was complete.

The resilient armadillo provides an appropriate emblem for Austin's music scene, which, in spite of growing difficulties, exhibits remarkable vitality. Forced into smaller, more costly, and less convenient quarters, nightclub owners and bands continue to produce excellent live music. In 1985 Nashville BMI executive Del Bryant could still tell Austin reporter Pete Szilagyi, "We feel strongly that the next star to hit the industry at any given time is likely to come out of Texas, and the greatest point of focus is Austin." Much promise; but will it come true?

The original progressive country movement has of course faded with time, yielding to the dominant styles of the eighties. Blues revivalists, hardcore country singers, and new wave artists all enjoy loyal audiences. Although the music may have changed, those audiences share with fans of the sixties and seventies the patented Austin enthusiasm. Belatedly, Chamber of Commerce and city officials have come to see that a thriving music industry greatly enhances the city's "quality of life" — and hence its commercial possibilities — and have taken a few halting steps to encourage its survival. The local scene continues to be a convenient reservoir from which Austin City Limits can draw interesting new acts. In its turn the series, now playing to over ten million viewers, has become a springboard whereby local acts can break into the national arena. Joe "King" Carrasco, Nanci Griffith, Joe Ely, the Fabulous Thunderbirds, the LeRoi Brothers, and George Strait are only a few local performers who have benefitted in recent years from ACL's popularity.

But of course ACL is more than a public relations gimmick for Austin and its musicians. It is a national show, a program that has made history. Playing ACL in its tenth year, a young Vince Gill, another singer associated with the "new Nashville," expressed gratitude at being on the

SEASON 10
1985

1001 Oak Ridge Boys
Bob Wills' Original Texas Playboys
1002 Neil Young
1003 Exile
The Maines Bros. Band with Terry Allen
1004 Waylon Jennings
Billy Joe Shaver
1005 Eddie Rabbitt
Tammy Wynette
1006 Ricky Skaggs
The Judds
1007 Glen Campbell
Eddy Raven
1008 Joe Ely
Eric Johnson
1009 Nitty Gritty Dirt Band
Steve Goodman Tribute
1010 Juice Newton
Mark Gray
1011 The Gatlins
Nanci Griffith
1012 Freddie Powers with
Willie Nelson &
Merle Haggard
Whitey Shafer
1013 Earl Thomas Conley
Vince Gill

**SEASON 11
1986**

1101 Gary Morris
Sylvia

1102 Mel Tillis
The Geezinslaws

1103 George Jones
Vern Gosdin

1104 John Schneider
Southern Pacific

1105 Tanya Tucker
Sawyer Brown

1106 Merle Haggard
with special guest
Freddie Powers

1107 Rockin' Sidney
The Neville Bros.

1108 Roger McGuinn of "The Byrds"
Kate Wolf

1109 Louise Mandrell
Mel McDaniel

1110 George Strait
Dwight Yoakam

1111 Legends of Bluegrass

1112 Songwriters Special with
Emmylou Harris,
Rosanne Cash,
& Friends

1113 Austin City Limits
Reunion Special

show and declared that the invitation was a wish come true. He said he had watched the program and yearned to be on it since he was a lad growing up in Oklahoma. If so, this kind of magnetism and its ability to shape a musician's development brings to mind the mythical power of the *Grand Ole Opry,* the *Louisiana Hayride,* and the other great long-running radio shows of country music's early days. Whether Austin City Limits will live up to such comparisons remains to be seen, but that Gill could make such a remark says much about a show that came shakily onto the television screen in 1976.

After so many years, Austin City Limits has amassed a body of work that holds great value not only for music lovers but for historians and folklorists as well. Cajun musician Michael Doucet's words are appropriate: "The musician is not necessarily a sequined star. He is an interpreter, a spokesman for cultural values." The hundreds of tapes in KLRU's vaults chronicle a decade's development of an American art form, from progressive country and other "outlaw" innovations of the early seventies, to Nashville's response, to the emergence of interesting syntheses.

Time can only increase the archival value of tapes by such pioneers of country, folk, and blues as Merle Travis, Lightnin' Hopkins, Robert Shaw, Joe Maphis, Elizabeth Cotten, and Ernest Tubb—not to mention the historic reunions of the creators of the Southwest's most important regional music, Western Swing. In effect the ACL tapes comprise a representative, if not complete, survey of country music from the 1930s to the 1980s. It is worth mentioning as well that, by taking the music from the dance halls and honky-tonks to the concert stage, the show invited consideration of country music for its value as art rather than as mere accompaniment to drinking, dancing,

or working. In this regard one might consider what happened when Cajun music, on the verge of suffocation by commercial country and western, began to be played at folk festivals in the 1960s. Once it gained center stage, and people listened to it, they found great aesthetic merit in the music, and a spirited revival ensued.

Country music has achieved enormous popularity since the dawn of Austin City Limits. Some of this appeal must derive from its bedrock position in American folk and popular culture, perhaps traceable to the romantic nostalgia that has affected so many since they pulled up stakes in Europe and Africa and came to the new world. For much of country music, including the Appalachian folk ballads and the gospel music of both white and black churches, has been a kind of pastoral literature, looking back to the past, to a more innocent golden age of rustic virtues and fireside charms, or to the beyond, to an unspecified happy refuge "far away" from care and sorrow. Such themes can still appeal strongly to modern listeners dissatisfied with their lives, their jobs or the way the country is going to hell in a handbasket. Country music can speak eloquently to other emotional needs as well: For example, a heartfelt song by a country musician capable of being "sincere" in the old style—Willie Nelson, George Jones, Merle Haggard—undoubtedly does more to combat the blues than any number of sugary pop confections. In 1980 San Francisco's KSAN-FM, a rock station that had practically walked point for the 1960s counterculture, raised eyebrows by switching to a country format. But, said the station manager, "Hillbilly is a more universal music. It's music for people who have grown up."

(What this says about Austin's KOKE-FM, the station that led the city's music explosion, is another matter. In the seventies KOKE irked its listeners by dropping "progressive country" for a straight "Sterling Country" playlist, then in the eighties abandoned country music altogether for something called "Lite-Rock." Like the trendily spelled beverage from which it took its name, the new format was at least 99 percent free of stimulating content.)

Of course, much of country music's expanded audience might also be attributed to the infiltration by country-pop of markets traditionally devoted to mainstream popular music. Some would question whether this was really "country" country music, though, for country-pop proceeded from an impulse to dilute country music rather than to "countrify" popular music. In short, it was a movement *away* from roots, and its decline in the eighties seemed to bear out the lack of wisdom in such a development. By contrast, great numbers of Americans have in recent years taken a fresh interest in the music, art, and handicrafts of vernacular cultures and subcultures, including their own—part of a quest for authenticity, perhaps, in an increasingly homogenized and technological mass society. This upsurge has doubtlessly contributed as much as any other shift in taste to Austin City Limits' longevity.

In its eclectic array of historical and regional music, with roots in the eddies and backwaters of American culture, ACL has presented a valuable alternative both to mainstream mass culture and to the Nashville hegemony over country music. It has directed national attention to regional music, Southwestern and Southeastern. Austin City Limits provided a window through which people could get acquainted firsthand with the Cajun, Creole, Mexican-American, black, mountain, and cowboy traditions whose elements, taken up and transformed, have for decades enriched the stream of American pop culture. Not only that, but such

events as the Texas swing revival shows, *conjunto* performances, and bluegrass jamborees served to renew the interest of many regional audiences in their own musical heritage. Especially for aspiring young musicians, the show provided important access to a usable musical past. In Texas, certainly, Western Swing has found new appreciation and vitality, thanks in large part to a momentum begun by exposure on ACL.

Austin City Limits played an important role also in carrying the Austin "redneck-hippie" blend of music and philosophy to a wider audience. If this was at first largely unwitting on ACL's part—the show just needed cheap talent, after all—its effects nevertheless touched a sizable percentage of American young people. Archie Green, in a scholarly article called "Austin's Cosmic Cowboys," asserts that Austin's musical renaissance, with its harmonious blending of two once-hostile subcultures, means much for a pluralistic society too often bitterly polarized by conflicting values.

By calling attention to America's regional musical forms, in fact by allowing them to speak for themselves, Austin City Limits has sent an implicit message that our homespun cultures are valuable and deserve to be treasured. Among other pleasures, these forms of expression allow us to "talk back" to our national culture brokers, whose standards may be seen every day on Madison Avenue, on the six o'clock news, or in the *New York Times Book Review*. Lightnin' Hopkins stood as far from Madison Avenue as Clifton Chenier does from the Nashville sound. Yet Lightnin' and Clifton both produced music such as people really listen to; and ACL's freedom to present such music constitutes a great strength. It's an alternative that distinguishes it from mainstream programming such as the Nashville Network which has no choice but to bow to the commer-

cially rewarding fashions of the day. In reflecting the musical interests of a culturally diverse community rather than the financial interests of a monolithic business establishment, ACL and PBS have enriched everyone.

Already in Austin and around the country ACL has its imitators and progeny. Producers of these shows, using tiny budgets and today's inexpensive video cameras, have adopted ACL's format to shoot uncountable hours of in-concert performances by local and regional musicians. To name just one such Austin outfit, "Dixie's Bar and Bus Stop" has captured whole days and weeks of Rod Kennedy's Kerrville Folk Festival—an important event for Southwestern musicians—in addition to individually taping numerous struggling young artists, some of them very good indeed. Joe Gracey and Butch Hancock, both veterans of ACL in different ways, are associated with "Dixie's." They expect to market "Dixie's" tapes as videocassettes or as fare for the community cable programs and low-power television stations springing up around the land. Some media critics feel that community cable and low-power TV represent a powerful response to the historical monopoly of network television, heralding a revival of American cultural pluralism. If—O bright hope!—such electronic cross-pollenization ultimately brings about a genuine social and musical renaissance, Austin City Limits will deserve to take a bow.

Del Bryant is quoted by Pete Szilagyi, "Music Encore: Austin Acts Rekindling Faded Magic," *Austin American-Statesman*, 18 August 1985. Michael Doucet is quoted by Barry Jean Ancelet, *The Makers of Cajun Music/Musiciens cadiens et créoles* (Austin: University of Texas Press, 1984), p. 149. The KSAN-FM station manager was quoted in Bob Greene's syndicated newspaper column in the summer of 1985.

1976 1977 1978 1979 1980 1981 1982 1983 1984 1985 1986

Alvin Crow

**ASLEEP AT THE WHEEL   RUSTY WIER   CLIFTON CHENIER
TOWNES VAN ZANDT   THE TEXAS PLAYBOYS   ALVIN CROW
THE CHARLIE DANIELS BAND   DOUG SAHM   MARCIA BALL
BALCONES FAULT   FLACO JIMENEZ   JERRY JEFF WALKER
STEVE FROMHOLZ   B. W. STEVENSON   AUGIE MEYERS
WHEATFIELD   GREEZY WHEELS   BOBBY BRIDGER**

Rusty Wier

Greezy Wheels

The Texas Playboys

Asleep at the Wheel

Augie Meyers

Marcia Ball

Doug Sahm

Balcones Fault

The Charlie Daniels Band

Bobby Bridger

Clifton Chenier

Flaco Jimenez

Jerry Jeff Walker

Steve Fromholz

Townes Van Zandt

B. W. Stevenson

Wheatfield

Gatemouth Brown

ROY BUCHANAN   WILLIS ALAN RAMSEY   STEVE FROMHOLZ
AMAZING RHYTHM ACES   TRACEY NELSON   LARRY GATLIN
WILLIE NELSON   EARL SCRUGGS REVUE   THE DIRT BAND
DELBERT McCLINTON   GATEMOUTH BROWN   ALEX HARVEY
GOVE   RUSTY WIER   JIMMY BUFFETT   DENIM   FIREFALL
GUY CLARK   KIWI

Rusty Wier

Willis Alan Ramsey

Kiwi

Larry Gatlin

Tracey Nelson

Willie Nelson

Firefall

Gove

Alex Harvey

The Dirt Band

Delbert McClinton

Amazing Rhythm Aces

Denim

Steve Fromholz

Guy Clark

Jimmy Buffett

Earl Scruggs

Roy Buchanan

Ernest Tubb

**LOST GONZO BAND   MERLE HAGGARD   GATEMOUTH BROWN
JOHN PRINE   THE TEXAS PLAYBOYS   JOHNNY RODRIGUEZ
KILLOUGH & ECKLEY   VASSAR CLEMENTS   THE DILLARDS
GOVE   DOC WATSON   MERLE TRAVIS   JESSE WINCHESTER
ASLEEP AT THE WHEEL   LINDA HARGROVE   ERNEST TUBB
MICHAEL MURPHEY   STEVE GOODMAN   MOTHER OF PEARL
JOHN HARTFORD   BOBBY BRIDGER   CHET ATKINS**

The Dillards

John Hartford

Chet Atkins

Doc Watson

Asleep at the Wheel

Mother of Pearl

John Prine

Johnny Rodriguez

Steve Goodman

Bobby Bridger

Gove

Gary P. Nunn (Lost Gonzo Band)

The Texas Playboys

Merle Haggard

Michael Murphey

Killough & Eckley

Vassar Clements

Linda Hargrove

Merle Travis

Tom Waits

NORTON BUFFALO   JOHN McEUEN & FRIENDS   TAJ MAHAL
NEVILLE BROTHERS BAND   DAN DEL SANTO   BOBBY BARE
HOYT AXTON   MARCIA BALL   LITTLE JOE Y LA FAMILIA
DELBERT McCLINTON   CATE BROTHERS   STEVE FROMHOLZ
TOM WAITS   NASHVILLE SUPER PICKERS   LEON REDBONE
CLIFTON CHENIER   DOUG KERSHAW   LIGHTNIN' HOPKINS
ESTEBAN JORDAN   ALVIN CROW   PURE PRAIRIE LEAGUE
TOM T. HALL   ROBERT SHAW

Nashville Super Pickers

Dan Del Santo

Elizabeth Cotten

John McEuen & Friends

Cate Brothers

Robert Shaw

Marcia Ball

Tom T. Hall

Pure Prairie League

Taj Mahal

Lightnin' Hopkins

Bobby Bare

Neville Brothers Band

Esteban Jordan

Little Joe

Alvin Crow

Doug Kershaw

Norton Buffalo

Hoyt Axton

Leon Redbone

Mel Tillis

ROY CLARK & GATEMOUTH BROWN   MEL TILLIS   JOE SUN
DON WILLIAMS   JANIE FRICKE   TEXAS SWING PIONEERS
SONNY THROCKMORTON   FLOYD TILLMAN   WILLIE NELSON
GAIL DAVIES   FLACO JIMENEZ   BETO & LOS FAIRLANES
CARL PERKINS   MOE BANDY & JOE STAMPLEY   RED LANE
BILLY JOE SHAVER   JOHNNY PAYCHECK   JOHNNY GIMBLE
JOE ELY   JERRY JEFF WALKER   HANK WILLIAMS, JR.
MARTY ROBBINS   SHAKE RUSSELL BAND   RALPH STANLEY
UNCLE WALT'S BAND   HANK COCHRAN   WHITEY SHAFER
RAY CHARLES

DAVID EBERHARDT PHOTO   **Butch Hancock, Joe Ely**

Gail Davies

Gatemouth Brown & Roy Clark

Carl Perkins

Marty Robbins

Janie Fricke

Don Williams

Beto & Los Fairlanes

Hank Williams, Jr.

Shake Russell Band

Willie Nelson

Moe Bandy & Joe Stampley

Jerry Jeff Walker

DAVID EBERHARDT PHOTO

Johnny Gimble

Ralph Stanley

Uncle Walt's Band

Riders in the Sky

**JOHNNY RODRIGUEZ   ASLEEP AT THE WHEEL   RAY PRICE
THE CHARLIE DANIELS BAND   WHITEY SHAFER   ALABAMA
BILL MONROE & BLUEGRASS BOYS   SONNY THROCKMORTON
MICHAEL MURPHEY   GEORGE JONES WITH HANK THOMPSON
THE SIR DOUGLAS QUINTET   PASSENGER   RAZZY BAILEY
ED BRUCE   JOE "KING" CARRASCO   RIDERS IN THE SKY
DAVID GRISMAN QUINTET   BOBBY BARE   WILLIE NELSON
GARY STEWART   HANK COCHRAN   RED LANE   LEO KOTTKE
LACY J. DALTON   TONY JOE WHITE   FLOYD TILLMAN
CHARLEY PRIDE   TINY MOORE, JETHRO BURNS, AND
JOHNNY GIMBLE**

Tony Joe White

Mandolin Special

The Sir Douglas Quintet

Lacy J. Dalton

Ray Price

George Jones

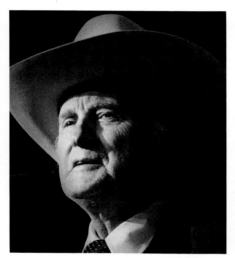

Bill Monroe

Hank Thompson

Alabama

Charley Pride

Michael Murphey

Leo Kottke

Gary Stewart

Asleep at the Wheel

Johnny Rodriguez

Bobby Bare

Joe "King" Carrasco

The Charlie Daniels Band

Passenger

Jethro Burns, Chet Atkins

GEORGE THOROGOOD & THE DESTROYERS   EMMYLOU HARRIS
LARRY GATLIN   ROY CLARK   TOMPALL & GLASER BROTHERS
THE MERLE HAGGARD SHOW   DAVID OLNEY & THE X-RAYS
RODNEY CROWELL   KRIS KRISTOFFERSON   RICKY SKAGGS
JAZZMANIAN DEVIL   PETE FOUNTAIN   CHARLY McCLAIN
TERRI GIBBS   THE BELLAMY BROTHERS   WILLIE NELSON
JERRY REED   CHET ATKINS   JOHNNY LEE   GUY CLARK
THE GEEZINSLAWS   GEORGE STRAIT   JOHN ANDERSON
DON McLEAN

The Geezinslaws

Larry Gatlin

Johnny Lee

Jerry Reed

Charly McClain

George Thorogood

George Strait

Tompall & Glaser Brothers

Guy Clark

Roy Clark

Rodney Crowell

Tomás Ramírez (Jazzmanian Devil)

John Anderson

Ricky Skaggs

Willie Nelson

Pete Fountain

Kris Kristofferson

Emmylou Harris

Terri Gibbs

The Bellamy Brothers

David Olney

Merle Haggard

1983
SEASON

8

Janie Fricke

T. G. SHEPPARD   DON WILLIAMS   EARL THOMAS CONLEY
JOHN PRINE   JANIE FRICKE   B. J. THOMAS
LORETTA LYNN   ROGER MILLER   DELBERT McCLINTON
WEST TEXAS SONGWRITERS SPECIAL   RODNEY CROWELL
STEVE WARINER   TAMMY WYNETTE   FRIZZELL & WEST
ROY ORBISON   MICKEY GILLEY   ROSANNE CASH
B. B. KING   RANK & FILE   JOHN CONLEE
CON HUNLEY   GARY P. NUNN   MICHAEL MURPHEY

Janie Fricke, Tammy Wynette

John Conlee

Keith Sykes, Guy Clark, Rodney Crowell, John Prine, Billy Joe Shaver, Bill Caswell

Roy Orbison

Delbert McClinton

B. B. King

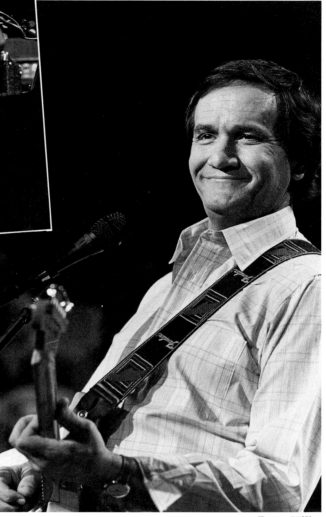

Mickey Gilley

Roger Miller

Gary P. Nunn

Townes Van Zandt

Rosanne Cash

Frizzell & West

T. G. Sheppard

Rank & File

Steve Wariner

Con Hunley

Loretta Lynn

Earl Thomas Conley

Bonnie Raitt

SONS OF THE PIONEERS   KITTY WELLS   JIMMY BUFFETT
THE LEROI BROTHERS   RAY CAMPI & SLEEPY LA BEEF
JERRY LEE LEWIS   FREDDIE POWERS   WILLIE NELSON
GARY MORRIS   JOHNNY RODRIGUEZ   NEW GRASS REVIVAL
STEVIE RAY VAUGHAN & DOUBLE TROUBLE   DOTTIE WEST
JOHN ANDERSON   DAVID ALLAN COE   LISA GILKYSON
LEE GREENWOOD   MERLE HAGGARD   GEORGE STRAIT
FLOYD CRAMER   BONNIE RAITT   THE KENDALLS
RAY CHARLES   GAIL DAVIES   THE WHITES   PEE WEE KING
THE FABULOUS THUNDERBIRDS   JOE MAPHIS   FARON YOUNG

Kitty Wells

Lisa Gilkyson

Jerry Lee Lewis

Ray Charles

Gary Morris

John Anderson

Lee Greenwood

Sons of the Pioneers

George Strait

Dottie West

The Kendalls

The Whites

Faron Young

New Grass Revival

Floyd Cramer

Pee Wee King

The Fabulous Thunderbirds

Jimmy Buffett

The LeRoi Brothers

David Allan Coe

Gail Davies

Stevie Ray Vaughan

Oak Ridge Boys

FREDDIE POWERS WITH WILLIE NELSON & MERLE HAGGARD
BOB WILLS' ORIGINAL TEXAS PLAYBOYS   EDDIE RABBITT
WHITEY SHAFER   NANCI GRIFFITH   THE GATLINS   EXILE
THE MAINES BROS. BAND WITH TERRY ALLEN   JOE ELY
TAMMY WYNETTE   GLEN CAMPBELL   EARL THOMAS CONLEY
VINCE GILL   NITTY GRITTY DIRT BAND   ERIC JOHNSON
THE JUDDS   OAK RIDGE BOYS   STEVE GOODMAN TRIBUTE
MARK GRAY   JUICE NEWTON   EDDY RAVEN   NEIL YOUNG
WAYLON JENNINGS   BILLY JOE SHAVER   RICKY SKAGGS

Whitey Shafer

Willie Nelson, Freddie Powers, Merle Haggard

Nanci Griffith

The Gatlins

Billy Joe Shaver

The Maines Bros. Band with Terry Allen

Earl Thomas Conley

Exile

Eric Johnson

Gary P. Nunn

Joe Ely

The Judds

Ricky Skaggs

Juice Newton

Waylon Jennings, Jessi Colter

Vince Gill

Eddy Raven

Nitty Gritty Dirt Band

Mark Gray

Steve Goodman (above left)

Eddie Rabbitt

Glen Campbell

Neil Young

Tammy Wynette

1986
SEASON
11

Tanya Tucker

**GARY MORRIS   SYLVIA   MEL TILLIS   THE GEEZINSLAWS
GEORGE JONES   TANYA TUCKER   LEGENDS OF BLUEGRASS
JOHN SCHNEIDER   SOUTHERN PACIFIC   ROCKIN' SIDNEY
MERLE HAGGARD WITH FREDDIE POWERS   GEORGE STRAIT
LOUISE MANDRELL   MEL McDANIEL   THE NEVILLE BROS.
ROGER McGUINN   EMMYLOU HARRIS   VERN GOSDIN
SAWYER BROWN   DWIGHT YOAKAM   KATE WOLF
ROSANNE CASH   REUNION SPECIAL**

Sawyer Brown

Roger McGuinn

Rockin' Sidney

The Geezinslaws

Mel Tillis

John Schneider

Mel McDaniel

Austin City Limits Reunion Special

Bill Monroe, Ralph Stanley

Gary Morris

Merle Haggard

George Jones

The Neville Bros.

Sylvia

Louise Mandrell

Dwight Yoakam

George Strait

Kate Wolf

Vern Gosdin

Jerry Jeff Walker

Southern Pacific

Gail Davies, Rosanne Cash, Emmylou Harris, Lacy J. Dalton, Pam Rose (hidden), Mary Ann Kennedy

This is a highly arbitrary listing, intended only to suggest a few albums closely associated with Austin City Limits and the Austin musical flowering. The list could easily be doubled or tripled. Serious discography-seekers are referred to John Morthland's *The Best of Country Music* (New York: Doubleday, 1984).

Austin City Limits Recordings

Bob Wills' Original Texas Playboys. *Live! From Austin City Limits.* Delta Records DLP-1164.

Clark, Roy. *Live from Austin City Limits.* Churchill Records CR-9421.

Earl Scruggs Revue. *Live from Austin City Limits.* Columbia.

Goodman, Steve. *Artistic Hair.* Red Pajama Records RPJ-001.

Nashville Super Pickers. *Live from Austin City Limits.* Flying Fish Records 097.

Nunn, Gary P. *Home with the Armadillo.* Guacamole Records GLP-001.

Perkins, Carl. *Live at Austin City Limits.* Blue Suede Records SLP-0002.

Other Recordings

Asleep at the Wheel. *Fathers and Sons.* Epic EG-33782.

Brown, Milton, and His Musical Brownies. *Taking Off.* String Records STR-804.

————. *Pioneer Western Swing Band (1935–36).* MCA 1509E.

Charles, Ray. *Modern Sounds in Country and Western Music.* ABC Paramount.

Chenier, Clifton. *Classic Clifton.* Arhoolie 1082.

Clark, Guy. *Old Number One.* RCA APL1-1303.

Cotten, Elizabeth. *Elizabeth Cotten Live.* Arhoolie 1089.

Crow, Alvin, and the Pleasant Valley Boys. *Alvin Crow and the Pleasant Valley Boys.* Polydor.

Ely, Joe. *Musta Notta Gotta Lotta.* MCA 815.

Fabulous Thunderbirds. *Butt Rockin'.* Chrysalis PV-41319.

Friedman, Kinky. *Sold American.* Vanguard VSO-79333.

Fromholz, Steven. *A Rumor in My Own Time.* Capitol ST-11521.

Gimble, Johnny, and the Texas Swing Pioneers. *Still Swingin'.* CMH 9020.

Haggard, Merle. *Tribute to the Best Damn Fiddle Player in the World (Or, My Personal Salute to Bob Wills).* Capitol SN-16279.

Hancock, Butch. *West Texas Waltzes and Dust-Blown Tractor Tunes.* Rainlight.

Hopkins, Lightnin'. *Texas Blues Man.* Arhoolie 1034.

Jennings, Waylon, and Willie Nelson. *Waylon and Willie.* RCA AYL1-5134.

Jennings, Waylon, Willie Nelson, Jessi Colter, and Tompall Glaser. *Wanted! The Outlaws.* RCA AAL1-1321.

Jiménez, Flaco. *Ay te dejo en San Antonio.* Arhoolie 3021.

McClinton, Delbert. *Victim of Life's Circumstances.* ABC.

Murphey, Michael. *Cosmic Cowboy Souvenir.* A&M SP-3137.

Nelson, Willie. *The Red-Headed Stranger.* Columbia PC-33482.

————. *Somewhere over the Rainbow.* Columbia PC 36883.

————. *Yesterday's Wine.* RCA AYL1-3800.

Professor Longhair. *Live on the Queen Mary.*

Ramsey, Willis Alan. *Willis Alan Ramsey.* Shelter SW-8914.

Sahm, Doug. *Groover's Paradise.* Warner Brothers BS-2810.

Shaver, Billy Joe. *Old Five and Dimers like Me.* Monument 7621.

Shaw, Robert. *Texas Barrelhouse Piano.* Arhoolie 1010.

Walker, Jerry Jeff. *Viva Terlingua!* MCA 37005.

Wier, Rusty. *Stoned, Slow, Rugged.* ABC Records.

Ancelet, Barry Jean, with photographs by Elemore Morgan, Jr. *The Makers of Cajun Music/Musiciens cadiens et créoles.* Austin: University of Texas Press, 1984.

Bane, Michael. *Willie: An Unauthorized Biography of Willie Nelson.* New York: Dell, 1984.

Flippo, Chet. *Your Cheatin' Heart: A Biography of Hank Williams.* New York: Simon and Schuster, 1981.

Green, Archie. "Austin's Cosmic Cowboys: Words in Collision." In *And Other Neighborly Names: Social Process and Cultural Images in Texas Folklore,* edited by Richard Bauman and Roger D. Abrahams. Austin: University of Texas Press, 1981.

————. "Hillbilly Music: Source and Symbol." *Journal of American Folklore* 78 (1965): 204–228.

Green, Douglas B. *Country Roots: The Origins of Country Music.* New York: Hawthorn Books, 1976.

Guralnick, Peter. *Feel Like Going Home: Portraits in Blues and Rock 'n' Roll.* New York: Random House, 1981.

Hemphill, Paul. *The Nashville Sound: Bright Lights and Country Music.* New York: Simon and Schuster, 1970.

Malone, Bill C. *Country Music, U.S.A.* Rev. ed. Austin: University of Texas Press, 1985.

Malone, Bill, and Judy McCulloh, eds. *Stars of Country Music.* Urbana: University of Illinois Press, 1975.

Martin, William C. "Growing Old at Willie Nelson's Picnic." *Texas Monthly,* October 1974, pp. 94–98, 116–124.

Miles, Emma Bell. "Some Real American Music." *Harper's Monthly,* June 1904. Reprinted in her *The Spirit of the Mountains,* 1905; reprint, Knoxville: University of Tennessee Press, 1975.

Page, Drew. *Drew's Blues: A Sideman's Life with the Big Bands.* Baton Rouge: Louisiana State University Press, 1980.

Reid, Jan. *The Improbable Rise of Redneck Rock.* Austin: Heidelberg Press, 1974. Reprint, New York: Da Capo, 1977.

Sapir, Edward. *Culture, Language, and Personality.* Edited by David G. Mandelbaum. Berkeley: University of California Press, 1949.

The Texas Humanist: Ideas, History, Culture 7, no. 6 (July/August 1985). An issue devoted primarily to Texas music.

Tosches, Nick. *Country: Living Legends and Dying Metaphors in America's Biggest Music.* Rev. ed. New York: Scribner's, 1985.

Townsend, Charles R. *San Antonio Rose: The Life and Music of Bob Wills.* Urbana: University of Illinois Press, 1976.

Tucker, Stephen R. "Progressive Country Music, 1972–1976: Its Impact and Creative Highlights." *Southwestern Quarterly* 2, no. 3 (Spring 1984): 93–110.

Willoughby, Larry. *Texas Rhythm, Texas Rhyme.* Austin: Texas Monthly Press, 1984.

(Boldface page numbers indicate photographs.)

Abrams, Todd, **59**
Alabama, **98**
Allen, Terry, 50, **122**
Allred, Sammy, 61
Amazing Rhythm Aces, 28, 30, **76**
American Federation of Musicians, 34
Ancelet, Barry Jean, 64
Anderson, Deacon, 47
Anderson, John, 54, **105, 116**
Antone's, 22, 32, 61
Archenhold, Mike, 8, 9, **56,** 57
Arhos, Bill, 8, **14,** 15, 16–19, 23, 27, 28, 30, 34, 37, 39, 40, 46, 52, 53, **56, 58, 59,** 61
Arnspiger, Herman, 21
Asleep at the Wheel, 22, 59, **68, 80, 99**
Atkins, Chet, 24, 34, **36,** 49, **79, 102**
audience: rehearsal, 7; studio, 8, 16, 19, 31, 32–33, 40–41, 51, 52, 57; television, 26
Austin Interchangeable Band, 19, 20, 30
Austin scene, 11–13, 25–26, 61–62
Axton, Hoyt, 44, 50, 58, **89**

Balcones Fault, 13, 25, **69**
Ball, Marcia, 11, 21, 24, 44, **68, 86**
Bandy, Moe, 50, **94**
Bane, Michael, 13, 18, 33
Bare, Bobby, 43, 44, **87, 100**
Bar-X Cowboys, 47
bats, 46
Baugh, Phil, 43
Bellamy Brothers, **107**
Benson, Ray, 22, 59
Berline, Byron, 41
Beto y los Fairlanes, 53, **93**
Blue Grass Boys, 46, 47
Boatman, Bob, 58
Boatwright, Bob, 35
Bosner, Paul, 14, **15**–16, 17, 23, 24, 25, 27, 28, 40, 45, 54, 57, 58, 61
Brammer, Bill, 39
Bridger, Bobby, 19, 20, 24, 50, **70, 81**
Brown, Bob, 12
Brown, Gatemouth, 31, **37,** 38, **72, 91**
Brown, Milton, 21–22, 24, 39, 47
Brown, Sawyer, **127**
Bruce, Ed, 10
Bruner, Cliff, 47
Bryant, Del, 62, 64
Buchanan, Roy, 31, **77**
Budweiser Beer, 59
Buffalo, Norton, 41, 44, **89**
Buffett, Jimmy, 31, 55, **77, 119**
Burns, Jethro, 48, **102**
Busby, Scott, 57, 60
Byerman, Mary-Margaret, 52

Caldwell, Susan (Susie), 49, **56,** 60
Calhoun, Fred "Papa," 21, 29, 47
Campbell, Glen, **125**
Campbell, Zeke, 47, 59
Campi, Ray, 48, 55
Carr, Patrick, 32
Carrasco, Joe "King," 48, 53, 62, **100**
Cash, Rosanne, 50, **112, 131**
Caswell, Bill, 50, **109**
Cate Brothers, 44, **86**
censorship, 26–27
Chalmers, Howard, 14, 27, 28, **29,** 39, 40, 59
Charles, Ray, **46,** 50, **116**
Chatwell, J. R., 47
Chenier, Clifton, **20,** 24, 25, 26, 28, 44, 64, **70**
Clark, Guy, 31, 50, **77, 104, 109**
Clark, Roy, 59, **91, 105**
Clawson, Cynthia, **58**
Clements, Vassar, 37, 41, 47, **83**
Clinch Mountain Boys, 46, 47
Cochran, Hank, 43, 46
Coe, David Allan, 13, 27, 35, 50, **119**
Coleman, Keith, 22
Coleman, Michael, 36
Collins Sisters, 48
Colter, Jessi, 30, **124**
Conley, Earl Thomas, **113, 122**
Conqueroo, 12
Cooder, Ry, 25
Cornsilk, Carol Fatton, 58
Cotten, Elizabeth, 41, 63, **85**
Country Music Association, 22, 30, 53
Cramer, Floyd, **118**
Crow, Alvin, 19, 21, 24, 25, 40, 44, 61, **88**
Crowell, Rodney, 50, **105, 109**

Dalton, Lacy J., 50, **97, 131**
Daniels, Charlie, **15,** 24, 26, 55, **69, 101**
Davies, Gail, 50, **91, 119, 131**
Davis, John T., 12, 18, 33
Day, Jimmy, 49
Del Santo, Dan, 41, **85**
Denim, **76**
Denver, John, 53
Destroyers, 53, 54
Dillards, 37, **79**
Dirt Band, 31, 41, **75, 124**
Domino, Fats, 42
Double Trouble, 53
Doucet, Michael, 63
Duke, Charlie, 38
Dunn, Bob, 24

editing, 10, 23–24, 25–26, 45, 60
Egan, Mary, 25

Ely, Joe, 50, 53, 54, 62, **91, 123**
Emery, Michael, 9, **56**
Emmons, Buddy, 43
Exile, **122**

Fabulous Thunderbirds, 53, 55, 62, **118**
Filler Brothers, 19
Firefall, 33, **74**
Fletcher, Bud, 12
Flippo, Chet, 13, 18
Fountain, Pete, 48, 55, **106**
Freda and the Firedogs, 13, 21
Fricke, Janie, 53, **92, 108, 109**
Friedman, Kinky, 26–27, 44
Frizzell, David, **112**
Frizzell, Lefty, 26
Fromholz, Steve, 19, 24, 31, 44, 50, **71, 76**
Fuentes, Ed "Fast Eddie," 8, 9, **56**
fund-raising campaigns, 17, 51, 58

Gatlin, Larry, 31, 54, 55, **73, 103**
Gatlin Brothers, 53, **121**
Geezinslaw Brothers, 61, **103, 127**
Gibbs, Terri, 107
Gilkyson, Lisa, **115**
Gill, Vince, 62–63, **124**
Gilley, Mickey, 52, **111**
Gilmore, Jimmie, 50
Gimble, Jerry, 47
Gimble, Johnny, 35, 36, 41, 43, 47, 48, 49, 55, 59, **94**
Glaser, Tompall, 13, 26, 30, 39, 50, **104**
Goodall, Spud, 50
Goodman, Steve, 35, 46, 59, **80, 125**
Gosdin, Vern, **131**
Gracey, Joe, 13–14, 15, 19, 20, 21, 25, 38, 51, 52, 64
Gray, Mark, **124**
Green, Al, 58
Green, Archie, 64
Green, Douglas B., 11, 18
Greenwood, Lee, 52, 53, **116**
Greezy Wheels, 13, 25–26, 44, **67**
Griffith, Nanci, 53, 62, **121**
Grisman, David, Quintet, 48

Haggard, Merle, 20, 25, 37–38, 50, 52, 63, **82, 107, 121, 129**
Hall, Tom T., 13, 37, 43–44, **86**
Halley, David, 50
Hancock, Butch, 40, 64, **91**
Hargrove, Linda, 37, **83**
Harman, Buddy, 43
Harney, Greg, 17
Harris, Emmylou, 50, **106, 131**
Harris, Gene, 60

Hartford, John, 37, 52, **79**
Harvey, Alex, 30, **75**
Hattersley, Cleve, 25
Helm, Levon, 41
Hickey, Dave, 30
Hicks, Russell, 43
Hillis, Craig, 30
Hollinsworth, Curly, 47
Holly, Buddy, 21, 50
Holmes, Vance, 9, **56**
Hopkins, Sam "Lightnin'," 42, 43, 63, 64, **87**
Hough, David, 7, 9–10, 23, 24, 45, **56,** 57, 60
Howard, Harlan, 43
Hubbard, Freddie, 34
Hunley, Con, **113**

International Harvesters, 54

Jarman, Rufus, 33
Jazzmanian Devil, 20, **105**
Jennings, Waylon, 11, 13, 21, 30, 39, 50, **124**
Jiménez, Flaco, 20, 25, **70**
Jiménez, Santiago, 20
Johnson, Eric, 53, **123**
Johnson, Spider, 50
Jones, George, 26, 33, 48, 63, **98, 129**
Jordan, Esteban, 44, **88**
Judds, 54, **123**

Kendalls, **117**
Kennedy, Mary Ann, 50, **131**
Kennedy, Rod, 64
Kershaw, Doug, 44, **89**
Kesler, Estreya, **56**
Killough and Eckley, 38, **82**
King, B. B., 48, 55, **110**
King, Freddy, 43, 62
King, Jackie, 59
King, Pee Wee, 48, **118**
Kirby, Kip, 55
Kiwi, **73**
KLRN-TV, 13, 14–15, 17, 19, 27, 28, 34–35, 40
KLRU-TV, 40, 59–60
KOKE-FM, 11, 13, 19, 63–64
Kottke, Leo, 48, **99**
Kristofferson, Kris, 50, **51,** 52, **106**
KUT-FM, 39, 41, 53
KVET, 61
Kymmel, Augie, 15, 58

Lane, Red, 46
lead-in sequences, 17, 31, 61, 62
LaBeef, Sleepy, 48, 55

Lee, Johnny, **103**
LeRoi Brothers, 55, 62, **119**
Lewis, Jerry Lee, 48, **59, 115**
Lickona, Terry, 7, 8, 27, 35, 39, 40, 41, 42, 44, 45–46, 47, 48, 51, 52, 53, 54, **56,** 58, **59,** 60
Light Crust Doughboys, 21, 47
lighting, 7, 40, 46, 57, 58
Lipscomb, Mance, 43
Little Joe y la Familia, 44, **88**
Livingston, Bob, 38
"London Homesick Blues," 31
Lone Star Beer, 8, 59
Lost Gonzo Band, 20, 24, 31, 38, 44, 52, **81**
Lynn, Loretta, 39, **48,** 51, **113**

McAuliffe, Leon, 22, 35
McClain, Charly, **103**
McClinton, Delbert, 11, 31, 44, **76, 110**
McCoy, Charlie, 43
McDaniel, Mel, **128**
McEuen, John, 41, **85**
McGuinn, Roger, **127**
McKenzie, Martha, 27
McReynolds, Jim and Jesse, 47
Maines Brothers, 50, **122**
Majewski, Carlyn, 20
Mandrell, Barbara, 53, 54
Mandrell, Louise, **130**
Maphis, Joe, 48, 49, 63
Maphis, Rose Lee, 48, 49
Martaus, Dan, **56**
Menotti, Gary, 8, 9, 10, **56,** 57–58, **59,** 60
Metheny, Pat, 34
Meyers, Augie, **68**
Miller, Cliff, 36
Miller, Roger, 50, **111**
Miller, Townsend, 15
Monroe, Bill, 46–47, **98, 129**
Montgomery, Smokey, 47
Moon Hill Management, 30
Moore, Tiny, 48
Moorehead, Robert, 9, **56**
Morris, Gary, **6,** 8–10, **116, 129**
Mother Earth, 30
Mother of Pearl, **80**
Mounce, Bill, 47
Muir, Allan, **45,** 46, 57, 60
Murphey, Michael Martin, 11, 19, 20, 24, 35, 50, **82, 99**
Musical Brownies, 21–22, 29, 47
Myers, Billy Lee, **56**

Nashville Super Pickers, 43, 59, **85**
Neely, Bill, 26

Nelson, Bobbie, 12
Nelson, Tracey, 30, **74**
Nelson, Willie, 11, 12–13, 16, 18, 20, 24, 25, 29, 30, 33, 37, 39, 43, 46, 49, 50, 52, 55, 58, 59, 62, 63, **74, 93, 105, 121**
Neville, Aaron, 42, 44
Neville Brothers, 40, 42, **88**
New Grass Revival, **118**
New Riders of the Purple Sage, 49
Newton, Juice, 52, 53, **124**
Newton, Scott, **9**
Newton-John, Olivia, 53
Nitty Gritty Dirt Band, 31, 41, **75, 124**
Nunn, Gary P., 31, 38, 59, **81, 111, 123**

Oak Ridge Boys, 49, 52, **120**
Olden, Walter, **56**
Olney, David, 55, **107**
Orbison, Roy, 48, 59, **110**
"outtakes," 43

Palmer, Robert, 54
Passenger, **101**
Patoski, Joe Nick, 44
pay: for performers, 10, 21, 33, 42–43, 48; for staff, 24, 57
Paycheck, Johnny, 32
Perkins, Carl, 21, 48, 59, **92**
Peterson, Jeff, **56**
pilot program, 17
Pleasant Valley Boys, 21, 25, 61
Point, Michael, 37, 38, 42, 44
Powers, Freddie, 50, **121**
Presley, Elvis, 21
Price, Ray, 46, **98**
Pride, Charley, 48, **98**
Prine, John, 35, 46, 50, **80, 109**
Professor Longhair, 42, 43
Professors of Pleasure, 41
Public Broadcasting Service (PBS), 14, 17, 18, 26, 27, 28–29, 46, 52
Pure Prairie League, 44, **87**

Rabbitt, Eddie, 52, 53, 57, **125**
Rabourn, Dean, 19, 28
radio "simulcast," 24, 53
Raelettes, 46
Raitt, Bonnie, 48, 53, 55, **114**
Ramírez Tomás, 19–20, 41, **105**
Ramsey, Willis Alan, 31, 33, **73**
Rank and File, 54, **112**
Raven, Eddy, 52, 53, **124**
Ray, Paul, 12, 18
Redbone, Leon, 40, **89**
Reed, Jerry, 58, **103**
Reid, Jan, 15, 29, 33

Reinert, Al, 32, 33
Reinhardt, Django, 59
Reneau, Frank, 47
Riders in the Sky, 11, 49, **96**
RKO All-Stars, 41
Robb, Doug, 9, **56**
Robbins, Hargus "Pig," 43
Robbins, Marty, 43, **92**
Rockin' Sidney, **127**
Rodgers, Jimmie, 26, 30, 35
Rodriguez, Johnny, 37, **80, 100**
Rogers, Kenny, 53, 54
Rogers, Lorene, 41
Ronstadt, Linda, 8, 11
Rose, Pam, 50, **131**
Rose City Swingsters, 47
Royal, Darrell, 13, 32–**33,** 38, 46, 50
Russell, Leon, 39, 48
Russell, Shake, **93**

Sahm, Doug, 11, 24–25, 33, 61, **69, 97**
Santee, Clark, 40, 45, 57
Sapir, Edward, 55
Savage, Bryan, 41
Scafe, Bruce, **14,** 17, 23, 27, 28, 31, 33, 34, 45, 58, 60
Schenkkan, Robert F., 14, 16, 17, 27, 32, 40
Schneider, John, **128**
Scrivenor, Gove, 28, 37, **75, 81**
Scruggs, Earl, 24, 30, 31, 47, 59, **77**
Sebastian, John, 43
Selby, Bob, 7, 31, **56,** 57, 58, 60
set design, 7, 15–16, 22, 40, 46, 50, 57, 58
Shafer, Whitey, 46, 50, **121**
Shamblin, Eldon, 47, 59
Shaver, Billy Joe, 39, 50, **109, 122**
Shaw, Robert, 40, 42, 43, 63, **86**
Sheppard, T. G., 52, 53, **112**
Simmons, Bob, 53
Sir Douglas Quintet, **97.** *See also* Sahm, Doug
Skaggs, Ricky, 47, 54, **105, 123**
Smith, Bobby Earl, 21, 25
songwriters, 49
songwriters specials, 46, 50, **95, 109, 131**
Sons of the Pioneers, 48, 49, **117**
Southern Pacific, **131**
Sparks, Hugh Cullen, 20, 22
Spirit Sound, 19, 28
Stampley, Joe, **94**
Stanley, Carter, 46–47
Stanley, Ralph, 46–47, **95, 129**
Steiner, Herb, 24
Stevenson, B. W. "Buckwheat," 16, 24, **71**
Stewart, Gary, **99**

Stewart, "Redd," 48
Stidham, Jack, 35
Storytellers, 44
Strait, George, 53, 54, 62, **104, 117, 130**
Strangers, 37, 38
Strzelecki, Henry, 43
Sykes, Keith, 50, **109**
Sylvia, **130**
Szilagyi, Pete, 62, 64

Taj Mahal, 40, 41, **87**
Texas Jewboys, 26, 44
Texas Playboys, 20–**22,** 35, 47, 48, 59, **67, 81**
Texas Swing Pioneers, 47, 48
Texas Troubadours, 36
Texas Wanderers, 47
Thibodeaux, Rufus, 54
Thomas, B. J., 53
Thompson, Hank, **98**
Thorogood, George, 53, 54–55, **104**
Threadgill, Kenneth, 26
Throckmorton, Sonny, 46
Tillis, Mel, 32, 43, 50, **90, 128**
Tillman, Floyd, 35, 46, 49, 50
Tolleson, Mike, 13, 16, 19
Travis, Merle, 36, 37, 43, 49, 63, **83**
Tubb, Ernest, 12, 13, 32, **35**–36, 39, 43, 49, 63, **78**
Tucker, Tanya, **10,** 30, **126**
Twitty, Conway, 54

Uncle Walt's Band, **95**
Urban Cowboys, 52

Van Zandt, Townes, 25, 50, **71, 111**
Vaughan, Jimmy, 12
Vaughan, Stevie Ray, 12, 53, **119**
Vaughn, Charles, 34–**35,** 39, 45, 58

Waits, Tom, 40, 44, **84**
Walker, Jerry Jeff, 11, 17, 19, 20, 24, 31, 38, 50, **70, 94, 131**
Wariner, Steve, **113**
Watson, Doc, **36**–37, **79**
Watson, Merle, 36
Wells, Jack, 60
Wells, Kitty, 48, **115**
West, Dottie, 52, **117**
West, Shelly, **112**
Wheatfield, 25, **71**
White, Tony Joe, **97**
Whites, 54, **117**
Wier, Rusty, 19, 24, 26, 31, **67, 73**
Williams, Bink, 10, **56,** 57
Williams, Don, **92**
Williams, Hank, 26, 31–32, 36, 49, 61

Williams, Hank, Jr., **93**
Wills, Betty, 21, 22
Wills, Bob, 12, 20, 21, 24, 30, 37, 38, 39, 43, 47, 55, 61
Wilson, Eddie, 13
Wilson, Kim, 55
Winchester, Jesse, 46
Wiseman, Mac, 47
Wolf, Kate, **131**
Woolley, Bryan, 54, 55
Wynette, Tammy, **48,** 52, 53, 54, **109, 125**

X-Rays, 55

Yandell, Paul, 36
Yoakam, Dwight, 54, **130**
Young, Faron, 48, 49, **118**
Young, Neil, 54, 55, **125**